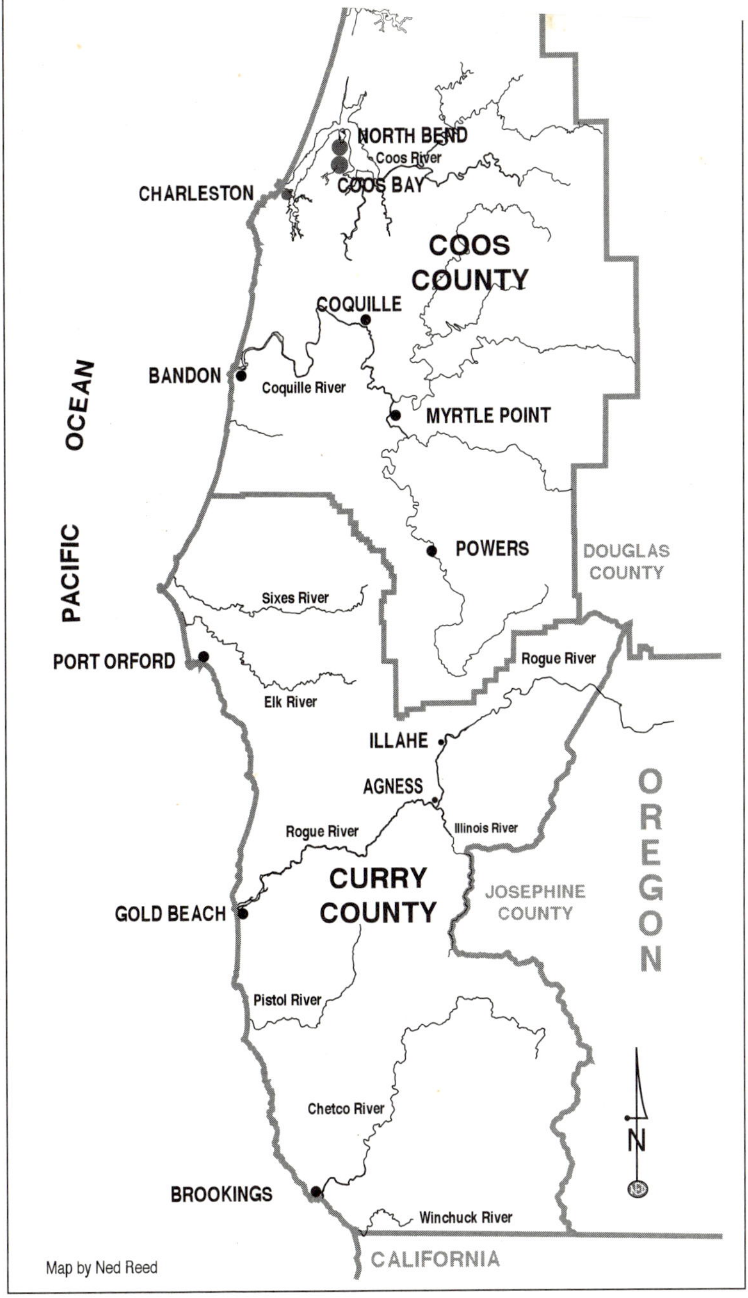

NORTH BEND
Coos River
COOS BAY
CHARLESTON
COOS COUNTY
COQUILLE
BANDON
Coquille River
MYRTLE POINT
OCEAN
PACIFIC
POWERS
DOUGLAS COUNTY
Sixes River
PORT ORFORD
Rogue River
Elk River
ILLAHE
AGNESS
OREGON
Illinois River
Rogue River
CURRY COUNTY
JOSEPHINE COUNTY
GOLD BEACH
Pistol River
Chetco River
N
BROOKINGS
Winchuck River
CALIFORNIA

Map by Ned Reed

WHAT HAPPENED HERE?

Stories and legends based on the history of Coos and Curry Counties, Oregon

to Clarence and Shirley

By Shirley Nelson

Shirley Nelson

WHAT HAPPENED HERE?

Book design by Jay Stoler

ISBN 1-892394-07-3

Printed in the United States of America
By Gorham Printing
Rochester, Washington

INTRODUCTION

When you visit a place, you never know who might have been there before you. If you visit the Oregon coast–or almost any other place in the state–you will walk where Native Americans walked. You might pass through forest or open fields where pioneer cabins once stood. You might pass the sites of gold or coal mines or mining towns, where nothing is left to be seen.

Long before Lewis and Clark arrived at the Oregon coast, seagoing explorers from Europe had visited it. Yet, it was the last part of the state to be reached by European-American settlers. People who came from the eastern part of the continent–the actual United States at that time–were looking for good farmland. They usually stopped when they reached the Willamette Valley.

The trip by covered wagon was long and hard, but it was much longer and harder to reach the coast by ship. Settlers who came by sea had to travel down the East Coast of North America and then through the Caribbean Sea to the Isthmus of Panama. They would walk or ride mules or horses through steamy, insect-filled jungle to the Pacific Ocean. Then they had to board another ship to come north to Oregon. Another way was to go around South America by sailing ship, a long and dangerous journey.

Settlement on the southern Oregon coast happened as it did in the rest of the United States and other parts of the world. A "first people" lived on the land. In our country we call them "Indians" or "Native Americans." They had lived here a long time and had their own way of life. People also came from other places, many from what was then the United States. Some came directly from Europe. They were looking for land, a new life, and a way to earn money.

At first, the Native Americans were curious, fearful, or both. The two groups got to know each other somewhat and perhaps tried to get along on the same land. More and more fights broke out and people were killed, both natives and newcomers. The newcomers were more powerful, with guns. They defeated the natives in war, killing many. They captured the survivors and took them farther north to another place to live. The newcomers changed the landscape by mining, cutting trees, farming and building roads and towns.

More and more people came, but towns did not grow as large as their founders hoped. Today it is still not easy to get to the southern Oregon coast, even though U. S. Highway 101 runs through it.

As you read or listen to these stories, try to imagine yourself as a Native American, watching strangers take over your land. Then try to imagine you are a pioneer settler, one hundred fifty years ago. Your family has brought you to this new place, by horse and wagon, on foot, or by ship. Maybe you have come part of the way by train. There is no house waiting for you. You and your family must clear land, build a house, plant a garden, hunt animals, and catch fish. You must do all these things without electricity, a telephone, or a car.

Many stories could be told of the people and events in Curry and Coos Counties. I have chosen these fourteen, to whet your appetite. The stories have been carefully researched, but some readers might disagree with some of the information. Capturing history is not easy because historical accounts do not always agree.

If you see a word you do not understand, you can look it up in the glossary on Page 100.

If you want to learn more–and I hope you will–the books in the bibliography have many more stories about the history of Oregon's South Coast.

Shirley Nelson
Port Orford 2005

ACKNOWLEDGEMENTS

My sincere thanks to these people who have been very helpful in reading and commenting on the manuscript, editing, finding pictures, and otherwise being supportive in the process of producing this book: Carol Acklin, Kay Atwood, Jessica Bryan, Andy Christensen of Bandon Historical Museum, Rick Cook, Jane Cramer, Eva Douthit, Nathan Douthit, P. J. Estlund, Laurel Gerkman, Theresia Hewitt, Don Ivy, Jackie Kerska of Curry Historical Museum, Ann Koppy, Tex Martinek of Gold Beach Ranger District of Siskiyou National Forest, Sara Mitchell, T. J. Murphy, Walt Schroeder and Vicki Wiese of Coos County Historical and Maritime Museum, North Bend.

TABLE OF CONTENTS

Face Rock at Bandon
Photo by author

Chapter 1

THE LEGEND OF FACE ROCK

Seatco, evil spirit of the ocean, caused the storms that blew up and down the coast. He killed fish and threw them on the beach. Sometimes he swallowed canoes and fishermen. The coast people feared him and tried not to anger him.

The mountain tribes did not know Seatco and so did not fear him. Whenever they came to the coast to trade, or to attend potlatches, they brought with them their families, horses and dogs; the children brought their pets.

One summer four chiefs of the coast Indians held a big potlatch in honor of Siskiyou, a powerful chief of a mountain tribe. The four tribes planned a big feast, for they wanted to show their guests how prosperous the coast tribes were. The potlatch would be held on the beach near the mouth of the Coquille River.

For days people were busy preparing the feast. The women and girls dug great numbers of clams and mussels and prepared them for steaming beneath sea moss and myrtle leaves. Hunters brought in a dozen elk and several deer. Many Salmon were made ready for roasting on spits over driftwood fires. Huckleberries were heaped on cedar bark trays. When runners announced that Chief Siskiyou and his people were a day's journey away, the roasting and steaming began.

The chief brought with him his beautiful young daughter, and they camped on the potlatch grounds. The daughter, Ewauna, had her pets with her—her dog Komax and a basket of baby raccoons. The girl had never before seen the ocean. All day long she and her dog raced along the beach excited by the breaking waves.

People of the village warned her, "Don't go alone on the bluff. Seatco might see you and take you." Ewauna laughed at their warning.

By the morning of the second day all the guests had arrived, and the great feast had begun. The four chiefs, dressed in their ceremonial robes, welcomed their guests and spoke in praise of the great Chief Siskiyou. All day the hosts and the guests feasted. That night they slept where they had eaten.

When all was quiet in the camp the great chief's daughter, taking her dog and basket of raccoons with her, slipped away to the beach. She ran and danced along the shore, singing a song to the moon, which hung low over the ocean. She danced nearer and nearer to the water, into the silver path. Then she dropped her basket on the beach, told her dog to guard her little pets, and ran into the surf.

She would swim toward the moon, following the silver reflection of the moon. Her dog barked a warning but she swam on and on, far from the shore. Suddenly a black hand passed across the moon, and she was seized by a creature that came out of the water. Seatco claimed her as his own and started toward his cliff with her.

Komax rushed to her rescue, carrying the basket of raccoons. He dropped the basket and sank his teeth into the demon's hand. Roaring with pain and anger, Seatco grabbed the dog and basket, hurling them down the beach. He held the girl close to him, trying to make her look into his eyes. But she turned her face away and looked at the moon. She remembered that Seatco's power lay in his eyes.

The next morning the chief missed his daughter. He and his hosts rushed to the beach. The tide was out. The girl was lying on the wet sand, her beautiful face looking up at the sky. Nearby, Komax stood as if barking. A little west of them were the scattered raccoons and the empty basket. All had been turned to stone.

On a large rock near the shore sits Seatco, still trying to catch the eye of the maiden. He too has been changed to stone.

ENDNOTES

Chapter 1

Several versions of this story are told. The first written version is said to have been set down by Ottile (or Otilie) Parker Kronenberg after listening to "Mary," one of the last of the Nasomah (Coquille) tribe, tell the story. Kronenberg was the daughter of Captain Judah Parker whom you will meet in Chapter 4.

Permission has been granted the author to use this version of the Face Rock story, published on pages 38 – 40 in *Changing Landscapes*, proceedings of the 5th and 6th annual Coquille Cultural Preservation Conferences. Copyright is by the Coquille

Indian Tribe, 2002. The writer was Jason Younker, University of Oregon Dept. of Anthropology.

The story appears in Ella Clark's *Indian Legends of the Pacific Northwest*. She also used Kronenberg as a source.

When you go to Bandon, go out on the Beach Loop Drive south of town. As you go south and look toward the ocean, you will see Ewauna's head, tipped back with her face looking up at the sky. Look carefully for her pets. There is a State Park near the rock, with paths leading down to the beach.

A local Native American leader has suggested that this story might have been a way to explain the great tsunami of January 1700 that struck the West Coast of North America.

Battle Rock at Port Orford
Photo by author

Chapter 2

WHAT JAYKEE SAW

Battle Rock - 1851

Jaykee, a young Indian boy, climbed quickly and quietly to the top of the huge rock at the edge of the sand. He went to the high end of the brush-covered rock, above the ocean. From here, his favorite lookout spot, he could see the edge of the deep-water bay to the west and the cliffs beyond. To the east, a curving beach stretched toward a mountain. He could see a long way south, out over the ocean. His ancestors had called the ocean "the river with one bank."

The day was sunny, the water sparkling blue. Jaykee saw what looked like the wings of a giant white bird, far out on the sea. He knew those "wings" were really sails on a large wooden ship. Wind filled the sails and pushed the ship over the ocean. Such ships carried light-skinned, often bearded men from far places. He had heard about the men from his elders. His bead necklace came from white men, who had traded the beads for salmon.

The boy watched the waves for awhile. When he was sure the sailing ship would not come ashore that day, he climbed down from the rock and went to his cedar plank home in the nearby forest.

Jaykee belonged to the Quatomah band of Indians. His people had lived on this coast for perhaps thousands of years. Quatomahs ate salmon and other fish, shellfish, deer, elk, acorns, berries, ducks, geese, and roots. In the forest they found wood for their homes and bark for clothing. They kept old customs, worked hard, and lived well. Their homeland was part of the area that became Oregon Territory in 1848.

On a June day in 1851 Jaykee watched from the shore as a ship came near the giant rock. Instead of sails it had a stack puffing steam into the air. The *Sea Gull* had come from Portland, a brand-new town in Oregon Territory, and was bound for San Francisco. The captain of the ship, William Tichenor, had met nine men in Portland and told them this would be a good place for a white settlement. He had said the Indians would not cause trouble.

John M. Kirkpatrick and eight other men came ashore in a small boat and landed on the beach. They started to unload tents, food and weapons. Curious natives watched. One of the white men motioned to them to come and help unload the heavy items.

The white men spotted the big rock with its low end nuzzling the beach. They decided the rock, with its grass, bushes, and a few trees, was a good place to camp. The white and brown men were partway up the rock when the steamship gave a blast of its whistle and sailed away.

Jaykee's heart skipped. This was something new; ships usually left with all of the strangers on board. This time some white men were still on shore, and it seemed that they planned to stay awhile.

Using Chinook jargon, the white men told the Indians who had helped with the work that they would be paid.

The natives were told to come to the rock when it started to get dark. The Quatomahs left the rock and the visitors began setting up tents, laying out their food and loading their guns, including one cannon.

Jaykee watched that evening as some of his people came to the beach. The men who had helped unload and carry the strangers' gear started up the sloping end of the rock. They climbed easily and carried no weapons. When they were close to the cannon, the nervous white men fired. Jaykee jumped at the loud sound. Smells of gunpowder and blood filled the air. The shot had killed several braves and wounded others.

Jaykee felt shocked, angry, sad and sick, all at the same time. Why did these white men kill his people who had helped them? Why were they here? What other bad things were they planning? Jaykee and the other Indians who were still alive hurried to their village homes. The white men's camp was silent.

The next morning, a few natives came to the rock. They wanted to bury their dead and the white men agreed to let them. Then they tried to tell the natives that their ship would come for them in two weeks.

Time passed while the white men waited on the rock and the Quatomahs watched them. Natives from other bands joined the Quatomahs. After two weeks, when the ship did not come back, the natives made plans to attack the white men on the rock.

The *Sea Gull* did not come back because the captain owed money and the ship had to stay longer in San

Francisco. The would-be settlers did not know this, but they knew they were running out of food and ammunition. As the natives grew more impatient, the nine white men left their camp late one afternoon. They took with them only what they could carry: guns, an ax, rope, and a few sea biscuits. Jaykee saw them walking and running northward.

Another ship arrived at the rock the next day. Jaykee watched several men come ashore and search the rock and the area around it. After awhile they left on the ship. What Jaykee didn't know was that the visitors believed natives had killed all the white men. When they returned to Portland they reported their belief to newspapers.

Meanwhile, Kirkpatrick and the others were travelling as fast as they could, on foot, through the forest, dense bushes, swamps, and on beaches. They tried to get as far away as possible from the angry natives.

Travelling was hard. The men had little food or sleep and they sometimes saw groups of Indians who might be unfriendly. They tried to keep close to the beach so as not to get lost but they sometimes went upriver or took other routes to keep out of fights.

Once a friendly native helped them. He showed them the pole that marked the boundary between tribes, and said they would be safe north of that pole. They met other friendly natives as they continued on their way. After some days they reached a white settlement at the mouth of the Umpqua River, about seventy-five miles north of Jaykee's big rock. It was their first chance to rest, find food, and recover from the hard journey.

From there they went by boat up the river to the little settlement of Scottsburg. Most of the men, still worn out from their experiences, stayed in Scottsburg to rest.

Kirkpatrick, according to an account written years later, went on by himself. He sometimes walked and sometimes travelled by riverboat until he reached Portland.

Portland was about as big then as Port Orford is now, around one thousand people. Portlanders were surprised to see Kirkpatrick and learn that he and his party had not really been killed by Indians. This “news” had appeared in local newspapers.

The *Sea Gull* later came back to Portland.

Back on the South Coast, the first try at white settlement had been stopped. Captain Tichenor landed a much larger group of men later in the summer, to begin the settlement that became Port Orford. People, mostly men, poured into the new town and into places farther south. They came for the gold they hoped to find along the rivers and in the black sand of the beaches.

Settlement and mining led to more conflicts with the Indians. The Rogue River Indian Wars lasted off and on from 1851 to 1856, with heavy fighting along the coast in the years 1855-1856. At the end, Jaykee, his family, and most of the other surviving Indians in the area were captured. They were sent to live on a reservation on the Central Coast of what is now Oregon.

Some captives went by ship but others walked many miles. The Siletz Reservation was far from the home the Quatomahs had known. Climate and living conditions were not the same. The people had not been allowed to take anything with them to their new home. Many died there, from hunger, exposure and disease.

The reservation was much smaller than the area where the tribes had lived. The United States government made it even smaller, several times. One hundred years later, the reservation land was all gone. Treaties accepted by the Indians, giving them some rights, were never approved by Congress.

After the natives were sent away, more white settlers came to the South Coast. Ralph E. "Jake" Summers was one of the nine white men who had camped on the rock. He later came back to the Port Orford area. As many early white settlers did, he married a native woman. She was Betsey, a woman of the Coquille Indian tribe. Their marriage was in 1856, the third to be recorded in Curry County. Their names and that of one son are carved on a gravestone on top of the rock.

We do not know if the Quatomahs had a name for the rock Jaykee climbed, but it has been known since the 1850s as "Battle Rock." A creek runs into the ocean near the rock. It was later named Gold Run Creek for the promise it seemed to hold for miners.

ENDNOTES
Chapter 2

Jaykee was not a real person.

This story is a combination of one that was told by Kirkpatrick and recorded some years after the battle, plus oral tradition of Native Americans. There are many versions of these events.

This chapter—in almost its final form—was read or heard and approved by several local people of Native American descent.

The Quatomah (or Qua-To-Mah) band was also known as Kwatami. They were part of the Tututni or Tutu-Tunne Tribe.

Every year in the fall, members of the Siletz tribes walk and run down the coast from northern Oregon to the Rogue River, in memory of the forced march of their ancestors. The people of Port Orford usually hold a potluck dinner to welcome them as they pass through the town.

The ship, *Sea Gull*, wrecked at Humboldt Bay in northern California in January of 1852, only a few months after its visit to Battle Rock. No lives were lost.

Native Americans have a story about the first ship to visit the Oregon Coast (the last story in Clark's *Legends*).

Captain William Tichenor, the driving force behind the settlement of Port Orford, commanded one of the ships that carried natives away from the area to the reservation. You will meet him again in Chapters 3 and 4.

If you visit Port Orford, you can see the giant rock at the edge of the beach. You might want to walk through the tunnel in the rock at low tide. People like to climb Battle Rock, but it causes erosion. Poison oak grows on top, so be careful.

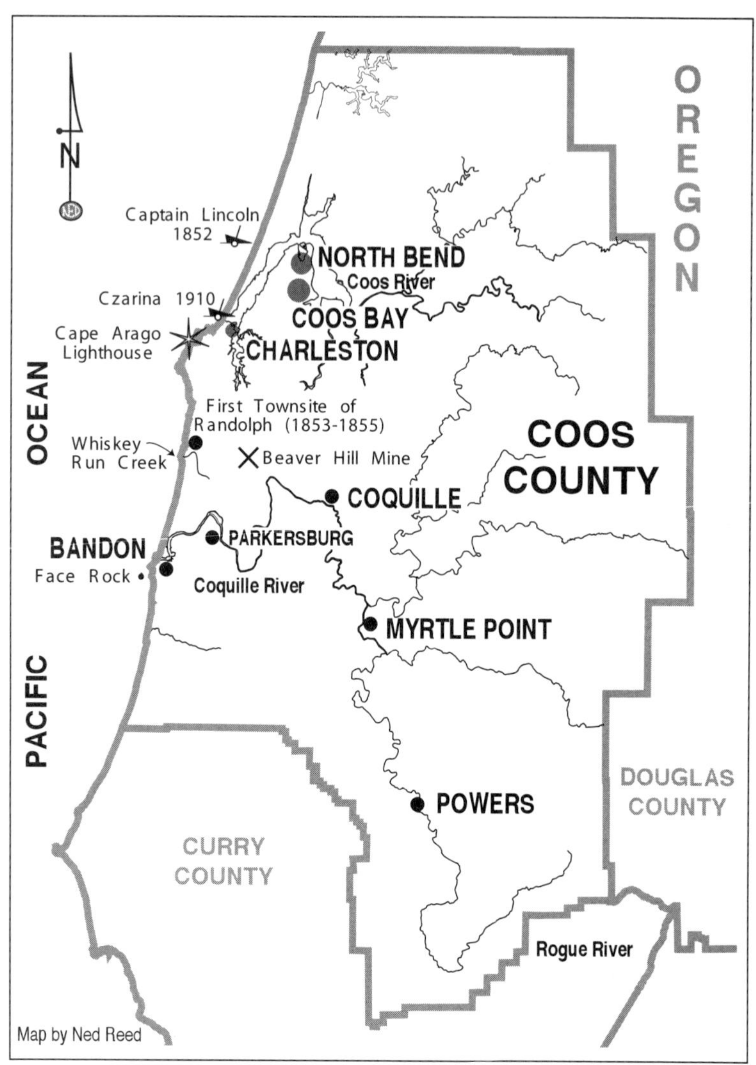

COOS COUNTY, OREGON

Turn back to this map to find mines, shipwrecks and other places in Chapters 3, 4, 5, 7.

Chapter 3

WE'LL BE RICH!

Using Natural Resources – 1850s to 1980s

"Tom! Tom, look what I found!" A young man in dusty work clothes ran to his cabin to find his partner. He held something bright and shiny in his hand.

"Tom, we were right; there is gold here, right on our claim! We'll be rich!"

Tom took the small nugget, turning it over slowly in his hand. A big smile spread across his face. "What are we waitin' for, Frank? Let's go!" He grabbed a pick and shovel and followed his friend back to their mining claim.

Early white settlers on the southern Oregon coast hoped to get rich. Some found gold, but few got rich. After the California Gold Rush of 1848-1850 and the discovery of gold in Jacksonville, Oregon, in 1851, gold seekers moved on to the Oregon Coast.

In 1853 men found shiny bits of gold and other minerals in the form of tiny flecks in the black sands of ocean beaches. They found gold at the mouths of Pistol River and the Rogue River, and at Port Orford and Cape Blanco.

A lot of gold was mixed with the black sand where Whiskey Run Creek flows into the ocean, north of the Coquille River. The town of Randolph quickly grew up there with tents, cabins, stores, saloons, and restaurants. Thousands of men worked along those beaches and mined thousands of dollars worth of gold. But in the winter, ocean storms washed the sand and its gold flecks away. Randolph had one or two other locations before moving a few miles up the Coquille River, on the north bank.

Men also moved up the creeks and rivers, looking for more riches. Johnson Creek, flowing into the upper Coquille River in the coast mountains, had gold, so a mining camp sprang up there, too. Gold miners worked on the Chetco, Rogue, Illinois, and Sixes Rivers, and on other streams. Some mines lasted for years; others for only a few months. Captain William Tichenor and Jake Summers, whom we met in Chapter 2, were among the men who searched for the shiny metal.

Gold miners worked hard. In beach mining, men lifted shovels full of sand into wooden boxes. Then they poured or "sluiced" water over the sand. The heavier gold sank to the bottom of the box, where it could be taken out.

In the mountains miners dug large amounts of ore with picks and shovels. Sometimes they used huge nozzles to shoot strong streams of water into the sandbars or hillsides to wash out gold-bearing ore. Then they put the ore into a machine called a "stamp mill." The mill crushed the ore so the gold could be removed. Mining was very noisy because of the use of water and the digging and stamping.

Gold mining along the South Coast lasted into the early 1900s. Some people started mining again during the hard times of the Great Depression of the 1930s. A few lucky ones earned a little money.

Coal was mined in Coos County from the 1850s until about 1920. Some settlers found and mined coal on their own land. Patrick Flanagan, who came from Ireland, mined coal in the Coos Bay area for thirty years, mostly as an owner of the Newport Mine. In the 1880s he had 350 workers. Big companies from other states controlled the larger mines. Beginning in 1854 steamships took coal from Coos Bay to San Francisco, making several trips a month. In 1896, the peak year, almost 90,000 tons of coal were shipped from Coos Bay.

The price of coal depended on the need. For example, people needed more coal to heat their homes in winter. The price also depended on transportation. In 1916 the railroad from the Willamette Valley reached Coos Bay. People thought it would help local business to be able to ship coal by train. But, not long after that, fuel oil began to be used more than coal for heating and for running engines. People no longer needed as much coal, so better shipping did not help.

Beaver Hill Mine, between Bandon and Coos Bay, was the largest of the coal mines. Many workers and their families lived in the town of Beaver Hill. Boys as young as thirteen worked beside their fathers and brothers.

Work in coal mines was hard and dangerous. Miners worked underground in the dark. They were more than 1,000 feet below sea level at Beaver Hill. After coal deposits were blasted loose from the earth, miners used picks and shovels to load chunks into rail cars pulled by mules. "Diggers" earned the most money, getting paid by how much coal they dug.

Workers inhaled coal dust and sometimes had to crawl on their hands and knees or stomachs. They could be injured or killed by falling rock or heavy wooden timbers or by runaway cars. Underground gases caused smothering or explosions.

An explosion at Beaver Hill in 1916 killed three men. In 1921 another blast killed six and hurt at least twenty. The mine soon closed and mining families left. The town of Beaver Hill lasted a few more years, then disappeared.

Huge evergreen trees covered the hills in Coos and Curry Counties. Early settlers cut trees to build their homes, barns, and fences. They also had to clear land so they could plant crops. Gold miners needed lumber to build sluice boxes. Coal miners needed buildings above ground and timbers below. Houses were needed for the towns that grew up around mines. Ships were needed to send the gold, coal and other products to other places to be sold.

In 1854 three men started a sawmill in Port Orford. By 1856 Henry Luce and Asa Simpson had mills at Empire and North Bend on Coos Bay. Thousands of board feet of lumber were cut each day. Simpson later owned seven mills and two shipyards in the area. For sixty years, Coos Bay was the center of his empire, which stretched from California to Washington State.

Out in the woods the big trees were cut, one at a time. Using axes, loggers would make a wedge-shaped cut, called an "undercut," on the side of the tree where they wanted it to fall. Then one or two men, using a long cross-cut saw, would cut from the other side until the tree fell over with a loud crash. Oxen or horses were used in the woods at that time to haul logs to a stream or railroad for shipment to sawmills. Logging was another dangerous job. Huge logs or limbs, flying steel cables, and accidents with saws or axes could injure or kill the loggers.

Early timbermen felt that they had the right to cut the big trees and that the trees would last forever. New trees were not planted after logging until many years later.

Trees cut for lumber were Douglas fir, Port Orford or white cedar, western red cedar, Sitka spruce, and western hemlock.

Douglas fir was good for building houses, barns, and ships. It was so useful for building so many things that it became the most valuable of all West Coast trees. Spruce was used to build airplanes during World War I (1914 – 1918). Port Orford cedar grows only in a small area, in southwestern Oregon. The wood is straight and strong, and it was used for such things as broom handles, arrows, matches, and houses. Many ships were built with the creamy-colored wood. William Winsor of Port Orford is believed to have given the tree and wood its name in the 1850s. Native Americans had used it long before then to make canoes.

Settlers built furniture from another tree that grows only on the southern Oregon or northern California coasts--

myrtlewood. A beautiful hardwood with fine grain and different colors, myrtlewood is now used mostly for fine furniture and souvenirs for tourists.

Lumbering grew in the late 1800s and early 1900s. Just as with coal, the lumber business needed markets. A depression in the late 1800s was not good for business, but sometimes bad luck helped. After the San Francisco earthquake and fire of 1906, lumber for new buildings was shipped there from Oregon. Lumber was also needed after the Bandon fire of 1914 and the big one of 1936.

Goods were moved in new ways in the early Twentieth Century. The Panama Canal opened in 1914, so ships no longer had to make the long, dangerous trip all the way around South America. After the railroad was built in 1916, sending goods within Oregon was easier.

Business boomed after World War II (1941 – 1945). Oregon lumber and forest products went all over the world. Coos Bay was called "the lumber capital of the world." Throughout the 1980s the port was the world's largest lumber-shipping port.

The Pacific Ocean was another rich resource with many kinds of tasty fish. Commercial fishing began in the late 1800s. Robert D. Hume's salmon cannery on the Rogue River was the largest business in the area. The cannery was said to have put out three-quarters of a million cans of salmon a year from 1880 to 1900. Fishing was also profitable at Bandon and Coos Bay.

Everyone, no matter what kind of work they did, needed food. In 1850 the U. S. government passed the Donation Land Claim Law. A man coming to Oregon Territory could have free land if he lived on it and used it for four years. If a man was married, his wife could have an equal amount of land. Many early settlers got land in that way. People started to grow vegetables, fruit, grain, sheep, cattle, and poultry.

From the 1850s to the 1890s, people of the South Coast mined gold or coal, farmed, fished, logged, and built ships. At the end of that time, the value of farm products was about the same as the value of logging, coal mining, lumber manufacturing, and shipbuilding, put together.

A few people became rich from gold or coal mining, lumbering, or salmon canning. Most people did not get rich, but their lives were better because of the things they found on or under the land in Coos or Curry County or in the ocean.

ENDNOTES
Chapter 3

Gold mining is still done on a small scale by a few people.

Little or no traces can be found of coal mining in this area, but names such as Coaledo and Beaver Hill are reminders.

The lumber business has decreased as trees have been cut over large areas of land. When gasoline-powered chain saws became light and efficient, they were accepted by loggers who were proud of their ability to cut many trees in a day. It has been estimated that one logger using a chain saw can cut trees ten times as fast as old-time loggers in two-man teams using axes and handsaws. (Gintzler) Logging is now done by huge machines which cut off limbs, fell trees, cut them into lengths and load them onto trucks. In a few places, where people are concerned about the environment, logging is done by helicopter or with horses, with smaller amounts being cut. Sawmills have also been streamlined so work is done faster by fewer people.

Three of the trees mentioned in this chapter might not be quite what they seem. Botanists have different ideas about them: Douglas fir is neither a spruce nor a true fir, writes Donald Culross Peattie in *A Natural History of Western Trees* (Bonanza Books, New York, 1953). According to *Trees to Know in Oregon* (Oregon State University 1950), it is not a true fir. Port Orford cedar, also called Lawson Cypress, is neither cedar nor cypress. Oregon myrtle is called California Laurel on the other side of the state line, but is neither a laurel nor a myrtle. All three Oregon trees are unique, beautiful, and valuable.

Hume's cannery closed in 1908. In recent years, commercial fishing has declined. Hume's idea of fish hatcheries is being carried on in several places in Coos and Curry Counties.

Patrick Flanagan, William Tichenor, Asa Simpson, R.D. Hume, and Judah Parker (see next chapter) were men who were adventurous, determined, and willing to try almost anything as they settled and developed the South Coast. All of them mined gold, went to sea, and tried several businesses during their lives.

Beaver Hill Coal Mine and Bunkers
Courtesy of Coos Historical & Maritime Museum

Logging with Oxen at Camp Arago
Courtesy of Coos Historical & Maritime Museum

Kruse and Banks Shipyard

Courtesy of Coos Historical & Maritime Museum

The *Western Shore* 1874-1878

Courtesy of Coos Historical & Maritime Museum

Chapter 4

BON VOYAGE!

Shipbuilding – late 1850s - 1945

Bang, bang! Buzz, buzz. Dennis Holmes watched a ship taking shape. He loved the sound of hammers and saws and the smells of new wood, paint, and turpentine. He counted about forty men working on the ship; they were using hand tools.

Dennis came every day to Simpson's shipyard in North Bend. He could hardly wait until the ship would be ready to sail in a few months. Maybe it would be another *Western Shore*. He smiled as he thought of the beautiful three-masted clipper ship. She was called "the fastest clipper ship of her time," and she made a record trip in 1876 from Portland, Oregon, to Liverpool, England in about a hundred days. She made two more fast trips before she wrecked in 1878. She was only four years old when it happened.

The boy dreamed of going to sea. Twelve- or thirteen-year-olds started as cabin boys. He would work hard and someday be the captain of a graceful sailing ship. He knew of the dangers, such as going around Cape Horn at the tip of South America. Ships wrecked, some when they were only a year old. Other ships had years of service, fifty years or more. Oh, the excitement of sailing!

Dennis edged closer to the growing ship. In his mind he saw the tall masts and white sails that would be added later. Maybe he would build ships, as Mr. Kruse and Mr. Simpson did. His father had told him that John Kruse took charge of building ships, but Asa Simpson made the plans.

Dennis knew that Simpson had sailed around the Horn, coming from Maine to the West Coast. Simpson had learned shipbuilding from his father. Most builders came from other places where ships were made, such as the eastern United States or Scandinavian countries.

I could learn, Dennis thought. As he left the yard late in the afternoon, he did not know whether he would be a sailor or a builder of ships. But he felt sure his work would have to do with the ocean.

It was 1879 and the first transcontinental railroad had been completed for ten years. But on the remote Oregon coast, rivers were highways and the ocean was the freeway. Many boys dreamed of going to sea and some did. But times were already changing. Clipper ships had been built to get cargo quickly from one port to another, often in different countries. Because they were built for speed, they were more likely to wreck. The great age of clippers lasted only about forty years, from before the 1840s to about 1880.

Both steam-powered and wind-powered ships sailed on Oregon rivers and the Pacific Ocean in the late 1800s. By the early 1900s, diesel oil and gasoline were used to fuel engines. Sailing ships were still being used in the twentieth century. Both kinds of ships were often improved.

The first ships built on the South Coast were made to carry lumber to far away markets. But lumber was needed to build the ships, so mills and shipyards worked together. They were often owned by the same people.

William Tichenor of Port Orford built one of the first lumber-carrying vessels, the two-masted schooner *Alaska*, in 1857. She was the only ship known to have been built in Port Orford.

The first ships used for business on the Coquille River were of the same type as the *Alaska*. Many were built locally. Then came the three-masted schooner. Later, someone put a steam engine in one of the ships and called it a "steam schooner." From then on, every wooden or steel ship that hauled lumber from Oregon or Washington was called a steam schooner, whether or not it had sails. Some ships had both; these were used a lot until the early 1900s.

Tichenor was both a ship captain and builder, as were Asa Simpson and Judah Parker. Parker had also come from the East Coast (New Jersey), arriving in Coos County in 1876. By that time, at age 47, he had sailed all over the world, mined for gold and tried to get treasure from sunken ships off the West Coast.

He built a sawmill and the first tugboat on the Coquille, the *Katie Cook*. The *Katie* served for over forty years, helping sailing ships get upriver and helping many ships get across the dangerous bar to the ocean. In 1877 Parker founded Parkersburg and a post office was started there.

Shipbuilding was a major industry on the Coquille River for five decades.

The *Louis*, first five-masted schooner to be built in the United States, was born at Simpson's mill in North Bend. She had a steamer hull and was rigged for a trip to San Francisco to get engines. But she sailed so well that the engines were never put into the ship. She was the first of her kind to sail around the world. The *Louis* lasted from 1888 to 1907, when she was lost in fog off the California coast.

Between 1875 and the early 1900s Coquille River steamboats shuttled between the towns of Bandon and Coquille. They carried milk from farms along the Coquille River to processing plants in Bandon and brought empty cans back to the farms. They also carried other freight and passengers. Children rode the riverboats to school because there were no school buses in those days. People went to church by riverboat.

The *Oregon* was the largest sailing ship built in the Northwest in 1905. A three-masted schooner, it was built at Prosper on the Coquille River. The rigging was damaged in a fire at the Parkersburg mill, but was repaired. In 1906 a gasoline engine was added to the ship.

Hundreds of ships were built at Coos Bay and along the Coquille River between 1858 and 1945. Simpson's yard turned out the most in those years. It closed in 1903.

Knud Vladimar Kruse and Robert Banks opened a yard in 1905. They built steam schooners for the lumber trade. When World War I started, Kruse and Banks had 200 workers. After 1917, when the U. S. entered the war, they had 500. During World War II they built minesweepers and tug boats for the U. S. Navy. Those were the last ships of any size built on Coos Bay.

Automobiles and trucks were used more, highways were improved, and the need for ships declined. The last important ship built on the Coquille was a 56-foot diesel-powered fishing boat, the *Pacific Belle*, in 1945.

ENDNOTES
Chapter 4

Dennis Holmes was not a real person.

A boy growing up at that time could have a career at sea, but it might not be the way he dreamed it would be.

You can drive to the site of Parkersburg, on the Coquille River, from Highway 42S or U. S. 101. A small county park a mile north of 42S has a plaque with information about Parker.

Chapter 5

"ABANDON SHIP!"

Three Shipwrecks 1852 - 1910

I. The *Captain Lincoln*, a three-masted schooner, lay on the north spit of Coos Bay. It was January 3, 1852. The ship had sailed from San Francisco, loaded with men and supplies for new army posts in Oregon Territory. The captain had planned to stop at the new settlement of Port Orford to visit the fort there. But high winds blew the ship northward, past the landing. After three days of storm-driven travel, the battered, leaking ship went aground.

When the sea had calmed, more than forty men left the stranded ship and waded ashore. They took all of the cargo from the ship: lots of food, paint, turpentine, soap, stoves, ropes, and other things. They found fresh water lakes in the sand dunes. The men began setting up a camp, using the ship's sails for tents and to cover the supplies they had saved. The flag from the ship was raised to fly over what they called "Camp Castaway."

Lonely and far from other people, the place had been visited only twice before by exploring parties of white men. A few farmers and miners lived to the north and to the south. Some of those settlers visited the camp; one was Patrick Flanagan. He had once been shipwrecked, himself. Native Americans visited, too. They traded fresh fish and game for clothing and trinkets.

Camp Castaway lasted about four months. Finally, the men were able to get to Fort Orford on foot. The rest of the ship's cargo was taken to the fort by boat. The camp has been called "the first settlement of white men at Coos Bay."

II. "Weather's getting worse," said the *Alaskan's* first mate.

"Aye," answered Captain R. E. Howes. "Looks bad." The captain knew the side-wheel steamer was not in the best shape to fight the huge waves and high winds. The ship had spent its working days carrying people on the quieter waters of Puget Sound and the Columbia River, not the ocean.

Captain Howes and his crew were taking the ship to San Francisco to be repaired in May of 1889. In late afternoon the storm struck, west of Cape Blanco.

"Water in the hold!" shouted a crewman from below. "Pumps runnin' well, but havin' a hard time of it. We've got leaks." The ship battled the storm for hours in the darkness.

Water and spray poured over the deck as the captain steered the ship through a very large swell. Suddenly, with a loud crack, a part of the ship above the port deck broke off and fell into the sea, leaving a hole.

"Lower all boats," shouted the captain. "Abandon ship!"

It was near midnight when sailors lowered four lifeboats from the wildly pitching ship. The first boat broke into pieces as it crashed against the iron side of the ship. The three others trailed behind the *Alaskan* at the ends of ropes. Crewmen in life preservers climbed into the rocking boats.

Some of the officers wanted to stay with their ship and refused to get into lifeboats. The captain tried to change their minds, but had to cut loose the lifeboats. The ship began sinking, stern first. Captain Howes and his chief engineer jumped overboard. They grabbed pieces of wreckage to help them stay afloat. Together, they watched the *Alaskan's* pilot house float by with three men clinging to the top of it. The engineer tried to swim to the pilot house but drowned.

The three men on the pilot house, plus the captain and two others, were saved. One lifeboat came ashore with ten survivors, but the other two boats were lost with all aboard. A total of forty-seven had sailed from Portland; thirty-one died.

III. In January 1910 the steamship *Czarina* left Coos Bay in stormy weather, bound for San Francisco. The Southern Pacific Railway steamer carried twenty-four people, a cargo of coal from Beaver Hill Mine, and lumber. As she crossed the bar, the ship met high waves which broke over it again and again. Seawater put out the boiler fire, making the ship helpless. She was pushed onto the sand just outside the bar to the south. Then she drifted along the bar to the north spit, where she settled.

Each breaker poured water and sand over the ship, making her sink deeper into the spit. Constant lashing of the ship opened holes in the decks. Parts of the ship broke off and washed away, including the lifeboats.

The men at the nearby Life-Saving Station were alerted. They rushed beach equipment to the scene, but the wreck was too far from shore for a line to reach it. Lumber that had torn loose from the ship floated around it. No boats could get near the vessel.

As the water rose higher and higher over the deck, the frightened crew and one passenger climbed the ship's rigging. They could hold on only a short time in the freezing wind and tossing waves. One by one, they dropped to their deaths in the sea.

People wondered why the captain had tried to cross the bar with the storm raging just beyond it. They watched from the shore for hours, unable to help the doomed men.

A tugboat and two steamships tried at different times to go to the *Czarina's* aid, but the wind and water were too strong.

Accounts differ, but twenty-three or twenty-four crewmen and one passenger were on board. All of them died except for one crewman who reached the shore.

ENDNOTES
Chapter 5

These are just three true examples of the many ships which wrecked off the southern Oregon coast in the nineteenth and twentieth centuries.

Wreck of the Czarina 1910

Courtesy of Coos Historical & Maritime Museum

Cape Blanco Lighthouse
Photo by author

Chapter 6

THE FRIENDLY BEACON

Cape Blanco Lighthouse 1870 – the present

Seven year-old James Hughes watched workers lay bricks in a rising tower. They were building a lighthouse just a mile from his home! His father, Patrick Hughes, had agreed to let the workers dig clay on his land. They shaped and fired the bricks right on the family farm.

James could hardly wait until the lighthouse was finished so he could see it beam its powerful light out to sea. In December 1870 the oil lamp was lit to warn ships away from dangerous rocks. H. Burnap was the first lightkeeper.

Keepers came and went and James grew up, going to school and working on his father's farm. In November 1888 he signed on as Assistant Keeper at Cape Blanco. He became First Assistant a few months later. James served more than thirty-eight years at the station. He had to wait until longtime Head Keeper James Langlois retired, in 1919, before he could have the top job.

James married Laura McMullen of Langlois and they lived in the brick keepers' duplex on the station, together with James Langlois and his family. In the late 1890s five Langlois children, two Hughes children, four parents, and a third keeper (unmarried) lived in the house. Every year the lightkeeper sent a report to Washington, D. C. Every year, he asked for a second house for keepers at Cape Blanco. A wooden house was finally built for the Head Keeper about 1909.

But James never lived in it. He had moved his wife and daughters to his ranch on the north side of the Sixes River, across from his parents' land. He took care of this smaller farm and travelled by foot or horseback to the lighthouse for duty.

After James retired from the lighthouse, he and Laura moved to the East Coast where he died in 1929.

Cape Blanco was the third lighthouse built on the Oregon coast. The first, built in 1857 on the sandy banks of the Umpqua River, was often affected by floods. It fell over when it was only six years old. The next lighthouse was built in 1866 on a small, rocky island at Cape Arago, near Coos Bay. In 1909 it was replaced by a second lighthouse, farther from the edge of the crumbling island, with a taller tower and better fog signal.

Cape Blanco is the farthest west point in Oregon. A dangerous reef lies just offshore. Winds blow fiercely there and storms sometimes last for days.

The cape is about 200 feet above sea level and the lighthouse tower is 59 feet tall. The beam of light shines out from the lens at about 250 feet, making this lighthouse the highest in Oregon. (Yaquina Head has a taller tower, but stands on a lower headland.) The light at Cape Blanco can be seen from more than twenty miles at sea.

Lightkeepers did a lot of ordinary and boring work. They cleaned and polished the lens, trimmed wicks, filled the oil tanks, washed windows, swept, dusted, painted, repaired storm damage—over and over—and, of course, kept the light burning during the dark hours. Keepers always had to be ready for inspectors who checked to be sure everything was spotless and worked well.

Exciting things sometimes happened. James Hughes saw storms and shipwrecks while he was a keeper. The tower shook during earthquakes. Sometimes visitors came to see the lighthouse, talk to the keepers, and maybe have a picnic.

Lighthouses helped sailors find their way and made ocean travel safer. But many things caused wrecks, such as storms, fog, failure of a ship's equipment, fire, and human mistakes. More ships used the ocean after the lighthouse was built. So the number of shipwrecks in the area each year stayed about the same, one every four to six years. James Hughes retired before electricity was used to power the light and turn the newer, slightly smaller lens, which was installed in the 1930s. The last lightkeeper at Blanco left in 1980 when the light, with its 1000-watt electric bulbs, was automated. Now it shines night and day.

In 2005 the light had been shining for 135 years in the same tower. This is the longest of any lighthouse on the Oregon coast. It if stops for any reason, an automatic beacon goes on. If the electricity goes off, a generator takes over. The lighthouse has survived storms, lightning, earthquakes, fires, vandalism, and fights between keepers.

Lighthouses are no longer needed for ship safety. Large ships use radar and GPS (Global Positioning System) to find their way. Yet, pilots of small fishing and pleasure boats like to see the light when they are out on the big ocean.

Lighthouses are a big part of Oregon's coastal history. Many people work to keep them in good shape and open to the public. In the spring of 2003, repairs were made at Cape Blanco to make sure that the light will keep shining for a long time.

Thousands of tourists visit every year. Most of them climb the sixty-three steps to the lantern room to gaze at the beautiful lens and enjoy the view. James Hughes would be pleased.

ENDNOTES
Chapter 6

James Hughes was a real person. We don't know for sure that he watched the lighthouse being built, but it seems likely. The rest of his story is true.

You can visit Cape Blanco Lighthouse from April 1 through October, most days.

The author is a volunteer tour guide at the lighthouse.

A third lighthouse was built at Cape Arago in 1934. It shines today with a modern beacon.

Chapter 7

BRAVE MEN OF SEA AND SHORE

U.S. Life-saving Service, 1892 – 1915 and to the present

Carl and Ray Sandstrom looked around the Coquille River Life-Saving Station at Bandon with wide eyes. They saw men in uniform at work. Two men checked the power lifeboat to make sure its engine was ready. Two others carefully looked over a "pulling boat." They had to be sure all oars and oarlocks were in place and all seams were tight. Another man swept the floor. Two men cooked a meal for the crew. The boys watched their father, Axel, fill oil lamps. Smells of oil mixed with smells of food.

This was a Saturday. If the boys had come on another day, the crew members would have been doing other things; they had different drills on different days of the week. On Tuesdays, for instance, they took the surfboat out over the bar, no matter what the weather or ocean conditions. On Wednesdays they practiced signals. On Fridays they practiced ways to rescue people from drowning.

The men took turns in the tower watching the weather and the sea and river. If the lookout saw a ship in trouble, he would sound an alarm. Then all the men would leave the jobs they were doing and launch one of the lifeboats. Their most important job was to save lives, and they always had to be ready. Sometimes the men could only wait, just as firefighters do at a fire station. Sometimes they had to **be** firefighters. Life-saving men helped in any trouble, on land or sea.

Carl and Ray lived at Prosper, forty miles up the river, with their mother. They did not see much of their father. All of the men in the life-saving crew lived at the station. Alex was allowed one day a week to go home, by boat or bicycle. The family sometimes came to Bandon, but visits to the father's workplace were rare.

The Coquille River Life-Saving Station, the farthest south in Oregon, was started in 1891–1892. The station was built there because the Coquille River bar—where the river meets the sea—was one of the most dangerous on the Oregon coast. From 1891 through 1910 fifty-five ships stranded there; two or three each year. Sixty-four ship accidents happened between 1868 and 1914 at that bar.

Even practice was dangerous at the Coquille. In the first year, three men drowned in a lifeboat drill when huge waves upset the boat. But the overall record was good. Between 1894 and 1910 two hundred thirty-nine people were saved and only two lost.

The first Coos Bay Life-Saving Station, built in 1878, was on a small, sandy beach below Cape Arago Lighthouse. One man was the keeper. He had to get volunteers from the mainland if he needed help. In 1892 the station was moved to the North Spit of Coos Bay, and there it had a full crew. The United States Coast Guard took over life-saving duties in 1915. The station moved to the other side of the river, near the town of Charleston. The last move was to Charleston in 1968.

The United States Life-Saving Service started in 1871 in New York and New Jersey. It later reached the Great Lakes and the West Coast. The life-saving men knew they must go out. They must try to rescue people on sinking ships, no matter how high the waves, strong the winds or dark the sky. They were strong, brave, hard-working men.

But they knew that even the strongest and bravest did not always come back to shore. The motto of the service was, "You have to go out. You don't have to come back."

Rough weather or the force of a grounding ship sometimes made it too hard for the crew to launch the ship's own lifeboats. In that case, the Life-Saving Service tried to get their lifeboats close enough to rescue people. Two kinds of boats were used on the West Coast. One was an open boat, powered by eight oarsmen and a steersman. This was called the "pulling boat." The keeper of the station was usually the steersman. These boats were used at least until 1915; after 1910 they also had gasoline-powered lifeboats.

The 36-foot model, designed by Charles McLellan, was the most common. Coast Guard boats got bigger and faster over the years, but the 36-foot boat worked well. New ones were built as late as 1956. The last one was retired in 1987 at Depoe Bay, Oregon.

Sometimes the men used a "breeches buoy." This was a life ring or buoy attached to ropes. A pair of sturdy short pants or breeches hung down from the ring. The breeches looked a little like cutoff jeans. The person being rescued got into the ring and breeches. He or she was then moved along a line by a pulley to shore. This could be a cold, wet ride, but it led to safety. Many people have been rescued in this way.

Between 1878 and 1962 a Lyle gun, named for its inventor, made more rescues possible. This gun shot a heavy rope line from the shore or a boat to a stranded ship. Someone on board caught the line and fastened it to the ship. The other end was tied to a tree or other object on shore or to the boat which launched it. Then the breeches buoy could run along the line.

After all the people had been saved, the Life-Saving Service tried to save the ship or cargo. Ships were often towed and cargo was often saved. But sometimes things were so dangerous that cargo, ship, or both were lost.

In 1915, when the Life-Saving Service became the U. S. Coast Guard, Alex Sandstrom moved on to another job. The Coast Guard built more stations, including one at Port Orford in 1934. The lifeboat station there was active until 1970.

ENDNOTES
Chapter 7

The Sandstroms, father and two sons, were real people.

You can visit the Port Orford Lifeboat Museum, April through October. The museum includes the original barracks and other buildings, and a 36-foot lifeboat that was used at that station to save lives.

In 1914 a part of the town of Bandon burned. The men from the Life-Saving Station helped with firefighting. In 1921 a fire destroyed some of the buildings. The station was moved to another place in town.

In 1939 a new Coast Guard station was built on the river at Bandon. The station was active until 1946. The main building, in traditional Coast Guard colors of red and white, is still there.

Fewer Coast Guard stations exist now because helicopters are often used in rescues. Helicopters travel faster than boats.

Man in breeches bouy
Courtesy of Bandon Historical Society

Life-saving crew rowing across Coquille River bar, circa 1890s. Rock train in background, carrying chunks of Tupper Rock for North Jetty.

Courtesy of Bandon Historical Society

Chapter 8

THE SACRED ROCK

Tupper Rock 1880 – mid-1950s

The huge, two-humped rock stood near the mouth of the Coquille River for hundreds of years. Made of blueschist, it was hard and solid. Blueschist is a metamorphic rock; one that has been changed by heat or pressure inside the earth over a long time. The people of the Na-So-Mah Indian band (Coquille tribe) believed the rock was sacred.

Natives called it "sae-tsik-na." Another name was "Medicine Rock." Some called it "Grandmother Rock" or "Grandmother Place," from an old story. A young girl cooked a sea animal for her grandmother. The girl was breaking a rule of her people, because women were not supposed to cook at some times of the month.

The old woman was blind, but she smelled and heard the food cooking. She knew the girl was doing wrong. In anger, she threw her granddaughter and herself into the ocean. There they stayed, forever, huddled under their blanket.

Another Indian legend said that pounding on the great rock could calm the seas. Sometimes the natives chipped small pieces from the rock to make tools.

White settlers moved into the Coquille Valley during the second half of the 1800s. The town of Bandon, just upstream from Grandmother Rock, was first settled in the later years of the 1800s.

John Tupper came to the area in the 1880s. He built and ran a small hotel called "Ocean House" near the rock. White people called the rock" Tupper Rock" and treated it as a novelty. Walkways were built around it, and also a stairway so people could climb to the top to see the view. The rock did not last long as a tourist place because other uses were planned for it.

As Bandon grew, more and more lumber, coal, and other goods were shipped to other ports. The U. S. Congress voted money to build jetties to make the mouth of the river safer for ships.

Much rock is needed to build jetties: many trainloads and bargeloads. Some kinds of rock are better than others; blueschist is one of the best. Maybe the Indians were afraid to say anything. Perhaps Bandon businessmen did not know of the Indians' beliefs about the rock or did not care.

In any case, the work went on, and Medicine-Grandmother-Tupper Rock was blasted into pieces. The pieces were moved by trains and barges to become jetties—long lines of rock and concrete chunks on both sides of the lower river. The breaking up of the rock began and continued in the 1890s and off and on until the mid-1950s as the jetties were built, repaired, and made longer.

The Coquille Indian tribe built a home for older people, called "Heritage Place," on the spot where the sacred rock once stood. A few large pieces of the blue rock stand at the edges of the parking lot. The people who live at Heritage Place can look at them and also out to the ocean. They can see the river flowing into the ocean between the banks built from Grandmother Rock.

The sacred rock as it stood for centuries.
Courtesy of Bandon Historical Society

Tupper Rock when blasting was being done for jetties.
Courtesy of Bandon Historical Society

Chapter 9

WHO LIKES CRANBERRIES?

Cranberries 1885 – the present

Susie Smith wiped her forehead with her sleeve. The late October sun shone on the cranberry vines. She felt hot, sweaty and tired. She had been here in the field, kneeling or sitting on the ground, for a long time.

Susie picked another cranberry and peered at it. It was round and red, about the size of a marble and almost as hard. If she were picking strawberries or blackberries she would eat them. But raw cranberries are crunchy and very sour. She wrinkled her nose.

"Mother," whined Susie. "How much longer? When can we go home?"

"Soon," answered her mother. "Our box is almost full."

Susie looked into her small pail, which did not have many berries in it. She picked a few more. Plunk! The berries hit the bottom of the pail.

Susie tried to remember how the cranberries tasted with the turkey last Thanksgiving. Mother cooked the berries with sugar, and the bright red sauce tasted good. But raw? Well, they could make strings for the Christmas tree. That was fun. Sometimes Mother let Susie drop a few berries on the floor. If the berries bounced when they were dropped, they were good. If they didn't bounce, they should be thrown away.

Susie saw her mother stand and pick up the full box. As she followed her mother out of the field, she tried to think about Thanksgiving. It seemed so far away. Maybe Mother would make cranberry sauce for dinner tonight.

Cranberries are native to North America; they grow wild in natural bogs near the ocean and the Great Lakes. When the Pilgrims arrived, they discovered the wild red berries that were enjoyed by the native people. Cranberries were probably eaten at the first Thanksgiving. It is believed that Lewis and Clark got wild cranberries from the Indians when they reached the coasts of what are now Washington and Oregon.

Charles Dexter McFarlin came from Massachusetts in 1885. He brought cranberry plants that had been developed from wild plants and started the first cranberry fields in Oregon, north of Coos Bay. In 1887 he had his first crop. The soil and weather on the South Coast were just right for growing cranberries, so the plants thrived. The berries grew to be large and red.

Other people around Coos Bay started to grow the berries. The first known planting in Curry County was in 1895. From 1909 to 1920 and after, the industry grew in the area around Bandon. It grew slowly but became important on the South Coast. Many beds can now be seen from Highway 101.

The berries were picked by hand for many years, by families like Susie's and by Native Americans. Wooden scoops with toothed edges were later used to pull the berries off the vines. The vines live and grow for many years, so the trick in getting the ripe berries is to keep from spoiling the vines.

In the 1940s Joe and Matt Stankovitch of Bandon and R. J. Hillstrom of Coos Bay invented a mechanical picker. A man could walk behind it, as with a lawn mower, and the machine would do the work of picking the berries. This upright machine was called the "Western Picker." It was later replaced by the Furford Picker, an improved model that is still used.

Cranberries are still gathered in the same way. Berries harvested using this dry method are sold fresh in markets or grocery stores.

Cranberries that will be made into juice, canned sauce or jam are harvested by the wet method. First, the fields are filled with water. Then a person drives a large machine called a "beater" slowly through the flooded vines. The beater shakes loose the berries which float on top of the water. As the beater does its work, it looks a little like a giant water insect. The bright red berries floating on a pool of water are a beautiful sight.

Four other states grow cranberries: Massachusetts, New Jersey, Wisconsin, and Washington. In southern Oregon the Coquille Indian Tribe grows organic, handpicked cranberries. Cranberry growers have the same problems as other farmers: weather that is too hot or too cold, or too wet or too dry; weeds, insects, disease, and mice. Deer like cranberries, too. Honeybees are needed in the spring when the plants are in bloom. It takes at least two years after planting a new field before there is a crop.

Since Susie's time, people have found many ways to eat cranberries. We still make cranberry sauce, which is quick and easy. You can buy it, in a can, made with whole berries or jellied. Cranberry juice is popular, plain or blended with other juices. Many recipes use cranberries. Dried and sweetened cranberries make a tasty snack. Best of all, cranberries are good for you.

But if you don't like them, you can always get a needle and thread and make strings of cranberries for your Christmas tree.

ENDNOTES
Chapter 9

Susie Smith was not a real person.

Beginning in 1947 the town of Bandon has held a fall Cranberry Festival with parades, many kinds of food containing cranberries, and fun things to do. You can visit a cranberry bog and learn more about this interesting fruit. If you drive on Highway 101 through Coos and Curry Counties in September, October or November, you might see some flooded fields with the bright red berries floating on top.

C. D. McFarlin Cranberry Bog North Slough 1898
Courtesy of Coos Historical & Maritime Museum

Harvesting cranberries at Fraser's Marsh near Bandon, 1916.
Courtesy of Coos Historical & Maritime Museum

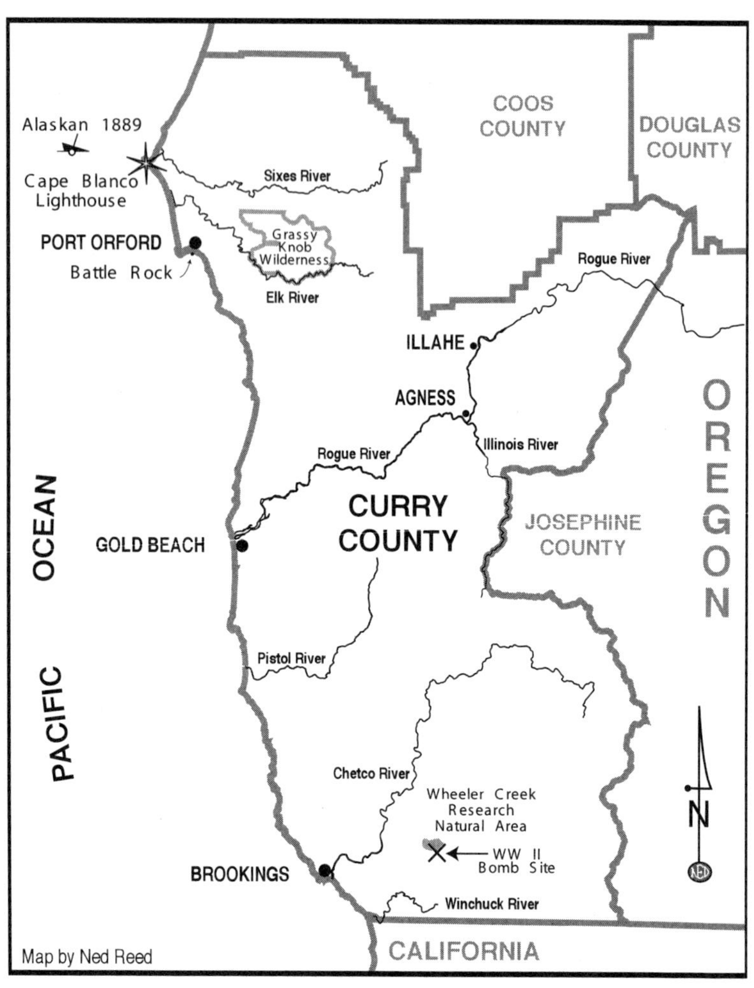

Use this map to find places mentioned in chapters 6, 10, 11, 12, 14.

Chapter 10

THE MAIL MUST GO THROUGH I

Mail Boats on the Rogue River 1895 – the present

Elijah Price held a letter in his hand. The letter had come from Washington, D.C., 3,000 miles away. It had taken weeks to get to him. Elijah and his family lived beside the Rogue River in southern Oregon, about forty miles from the ocean.

The year was 1883. Price had written to the United States government. He asked that mail be taken by boat to the people who lived along the river. Now the answer had come: "No."

When gold was discovered in Oregon in the 1850s people moved out into the forest. They lived along rivers and up creek canyons, far from any Post Office. By 1880 about fifteen families lived along the lower Rogue, which flows into the Pacific Ocean at Gold Beach. (The town was called Ellensburg, named for Captain William Tichenor's daughter, until 1890.) The settlers took turns making trips to town for supplies and mail. They floated downstream in a small boat, then rowed or "poled" back home. Sometimes they walked, or they rode horses or mules on steep, narrow trails. Both ways of getting to town and back were hard work. In 1883 the U. S. government did not want to send mail to so few people living in a wilderness. But Elijah would not give up. He worked with an Oregon Congressman who tried for twelve years to get government help.

In 1895 Guglielmo Marconi invented the telegraph. But people in the Rogue River Canyon still needed ordinary mail. Price wrote again in 1895. The new U.S. postmaster answered that they should try a mail boat for one year. He said there should be an upriver Post Office. Elijah's own log cabin became the Post Office and he the postmaster. Elijah was also told to find boatmen for the mail boat. There would not be any pay for Elijah or the boatmen.

The new Post Office was called "Illahe," which is Indian for "beautiful land." It was more than forty miles from the town and Post Office at the river's mouth. It took two days to row, pole, push, or "line" the boat upriver. To line was to pull the boat with a rope. It took one and one-half days to come back downstream.

When the river people found out about the new weekly mail service, more mail started to go in both directions. After a seven months trial period, the government started a regular mail route on the Rogue. In 1897 a Post Office, Agness, was set up at the place where the Illinois River flows into the Rogue. This is about thirty-two miles from the ocean.

By 1910 three boats, powered by gasoline motors, were used. It was still hard work to get upstream, especially in stretches of low water. But now mail could get from the coast to Agness in one long day. The trip back would be the next day. In 1907 three-times-a-week trips had begun.

It cost two cents to mail a letter. In 1930 mail was delivered daily, except Sundays. In winter, with higher water and earlier darkness, the overnight schedule was used.

Mail boats carried other things, too: groceries, household goods, freight and people. Through the 1930s, 1940s and 1950s passenger business swelled. Movie stars and other famous people rode the mail boats. Sometimes animals rode to farms upriver or markets downriver: including chickens, turkeys, rabbits, sheep, cows, and pigs.

Some animals didn't want a boat ride, such as the black cow who made the trip hard for everyone. She made the trip—against her will—in about 1925. An Agness family purchased the cow from someone in Gold Beach. The cow kicked, lunged and bellowed in the process of getting on the boat, again when men tried to get her off, and during the whole trip in between.

The mail boats took materials for three different suspension bridges up to Agness. The first was a footbridge in 1917. One for horses and wagons was built in 1924. A larger steel bridge for cars was built in 1932, but it was wrecked by a big flood in 1964.

A car went up the river—and back down—on a mail boat in 1928. A 16,000-pound tractor made the trip in 1933. All of the lumber, plumbing, roofing, and other material for a riverside lodge went by several boat trips in 1930.

Mail boat pilots have taken people downriver to doctors or hospitals and taken doctors upriver. They have rescued people from floods and saved others from drowning. In the late 1940s fourteen boats were in service. In 1959 the first jet-powered boat joined the fleet.

Eight blue boats still carry mail six days a week, all year long. The newest boat was built for the one hundredth anniversary of the mail boats in 1995. It is not jet-powered, but it is a replica of a 1940s mail boat and runs with a gasoline engine. Its name? *Elijah H. Price*, for the man who worked so hard and finally got the mail through.

ENDNOTES
Chapter 10

Today you can drive forty miles up the Rogue and beyond. But thousands of people come every year from all over the world to ride with the mail. They jet up the river, past many riffles, holes and creeks. These places have names such as Lobster Creek Riffle, Bear Canyon, Panther Creek and Crooked Riffle. After lunch and a rest, the people go back to Gold Beach. Riders might see wild creatures such as deer, elk, bear, cougar, bobcat, muskrat, otter, beaver, or turtle. They might see a turkey vulture, osprey, egret, bald eagle, great blue heron, ducks, or cormorants. Near the ocean they might see seals, sea lions or a whale.

Most of the material for this chapter came from *Whitewater Mailmen* by Gary and Gloria Meier.

Early Rogue River Mail Boat Circa 1910.
Courtesy of Curry Historical Museum

Modern jet boat carrying mail and passengers.
Courtesy of Curry Historical Museum

Hathaway Jones, mail carrier and master storyteller.
Photo from Illahe: Story of Settlement in the Rogue River Canyon. Original from the Glen Wooldridge Collection.

Chapter 11

THE MAIL MUST GO THROUGH II

"Oregon's Biggest Liar"
Hathaway Jones 1870 - 1937

Hathaway Jones was an odd-looking man. He was short, but had long arms that hung down to his knees. He walked with a stoop. A dark, bushy moustache hid his harelip, and dark-rimmed glasses framed his eyes.

His face was serious, almost sad. But a slight upturn at the corners of his mouth and a twinkle in his eyes showed the sense of humor that helped him tell tall tales with a straight, or "deadpan," face. He talked about the deer that ran around in circles and got hit by the same bullet sixteen times. He told how stubborn mules can be.

Hathaway's life did not give him a sense of humor. His parents divorced when he was thirteen. Later, his father took him to the Rogue River Canyon where they worked at mining. They joined more than 160 people living in or near the canyon in the 1880s. They were more than fifty miles from the ocean. There were no roads.

To get in or out of the area and reach a town, people walked or rode horses or mules over steep, narrow trails. Mail was carried on the backs of people or animals. Other things shipped in that way were flour, grain and feed for animals, wire fencing, fruit trees, or anything else that settlers needed. Mail and goods did not travel often into the wilderness.

White settlement of the Rogue River country began with mining in the 1850s. Miners and a few soldiers—who were there because of trouble between the miners and Native Americans—used the trail from Ellensburg to travel up the river.

From the east, goods and mail were taken from Roseburg or Grants Pass to Camas Valley. Then they went over the mountains by pack train to Mule Creek. The pack trip usually took two days.

By the time Hathaway and his father settled near the river, changes were coming. The Oregon and California Railroad put a station at West Fork in Douglas County in 1882. Some people wanted a route from West Fork all the way to the ocean. Miners and packers who lived in the area laid out a trail from West Fork to Mule Creek. It was finished in the 1890s. That trail was about twenty-one miles long and could be covered in seven or eight hours by pack train.

In 1883 Elijah Price started working to get mail delivered on the lower river. In 1889 Hathaway began packing mail along the mountain trails, working for a contractor. Price got his Post Office at Illahe in 1895 and mail boat service was started from Gold Beach to Agness, five miles below Illahe.

In 1896 a Post Office, called Dothan, was added at West Fork. A Post Office was started at Agness the next year. Jim Calvert was the first contractor between Dothan and Agness, about forty miles apart. He did not have the job for long; he died in a snowstorm in the mountains along the route.

Pack trains were using the trail often by 1898. It was the main route for visitors, hunters, miners, and mail. George Billings, who lived on a ranch on lower Mule Creek, started a trading company. It was the only place to get supplies between West Fork and the mouth of the river, a distance of about eighty miles. That same year, Hathaway got his own contract for the eastern end of the mail route, from Dothan to Illahe. He was twenty-eight years old.

Mail contractors lived hard lives. They carried the mail and other goods in all kinds of weather. Summer days got very hot in the Rogue canyon. In winter, snow fell in the mountains. The narrow, steep trails were often on the edges of cliffs. Rolling rocks were a danger, as well as rattlesnakes and bears.

Hathaway spent a lot of time alone with his animals and his thoughts. He studied nature and liked to hunt. Nature and hunting gave him a lot of ideas for stories. He also put his father, grandfather, and other family members into his tales.

When he made a stop, the mail carrier brought news from other places. He had a chance to talk to other men. They told and traded stories. With ideas from others and his own, Hathaway built a big collection of stories. He put his own special twist on them.

Here are two of the stories that have been saved:

The Slow Bullet (Version II)

One morning Hathaway stepped to his back door to throw out the dishwater when, glancing up the mountain across the canyon, he saw a big buck standing upon a high point of rocks. It was about two miles away, but he could see it clearly, could even count all five points on each of its horns. The air was very clear that morning.

Needing meat, he fetched out Old Betsy, took a rest across the back fence, and fired a shot at the buck. But after the smoke blew away he saw the buck still standing there as though nothing had happened. Then, seeking to reload for another shot, he discovered he was out of shells.

He stood there looking at the buck for quite a while, wondering what to do, when there flashed into his mind the fact that he had a small pistol which would shoot. Taking the pistol, he sneaked through the brush and up the mountain until he gained a position which was not more than twenty feet from the buck. Aiming the pistol with great care, he was just pressing the trigger when "thud," the bullet from Old Betsy hit the deer and killed it dead.

The Trials of Hathaway (Version I)

"My wife Florey said to me," Hathaway would begin, 'you better go out and shoot us a deer. We haven't got a bit of meat in the cabin for breakfast.' I hadn't gone but a little piece before I shot a five hundred-pound bear. That bear was the fattest thing you ever saw. The grease run right out the bullet hole and down the hill for fifty feet. I threw him on my mule and started home. Part way along I come across a deer. So I shot him, too, threw him up on top the bear and packed on down to the river. And then that durned old mule balked. Seeing how I couldn't get him to cross, I threw the deer and the bear on my back and started swimming. Halfway over, I noticed I was swimming deeper than usual, and I looked round. You know, that darned mule was setting up on top the bear."

Jones was not the only mail contractor in the area. Some others were Frank Thornton, Jim Thornton, Jake Frye, and Dean Walker. The Rogue River mail carriers were not as well known as the Pony Express riders, but they were much like them. They were young—many started the work as teenagers—strong, dedicated, and with a sense of adventure. Life was lonely while they were working. Hathaway married and had a son and daughter. They lived deep in the wilderness. His wife left him, adding to his loneliness.

Hathaway packed mail for nearly fifty years. In 1937, when he was sixty-seven, he fell to his death in a canyon near Illahe. He was on the job at the time. No one knows whether his mule threw him or the saddle slipped.

Jones was not the only teller of tall tales. Two others were John Fitzhugh, who also sang ballads, and John Fry. But Jones was given the title, "Biggest Liar in Oregon," which he held for several years and greatly enjoyed. He is remembered today by the people of Gold Beach. A Hathaway Jones Festival is held there every October, the month of his birth. People try to win the title of Best Teller of Tall Tales. But it's hard to beat The Biggest Liar in Oregon.

ENDNOTES
Chapter 11

The west fork of Cow Creek flows eastward into the main creek. Then it goes northeastward to join the South Umpqua River. You can drive there now, on a paved road between Glendale and Riddle. It is a pretty drive along the creek with the railroad running beside it. A bridge crosses the creek and a road leads into the mountains, following the route of the old pack trail. No buildings stand where once were a railroad station, a hotel, and a barn.

The two "tall tales" of Hathaway Jones in this chapter were reprinted from *Tall Tales of the Rogue River: The Yarns of Hathaway Jones*, edited by Stephen Dow Beckham, published by the Oregon State University Press, 1991. Permission granted by OSU Press.

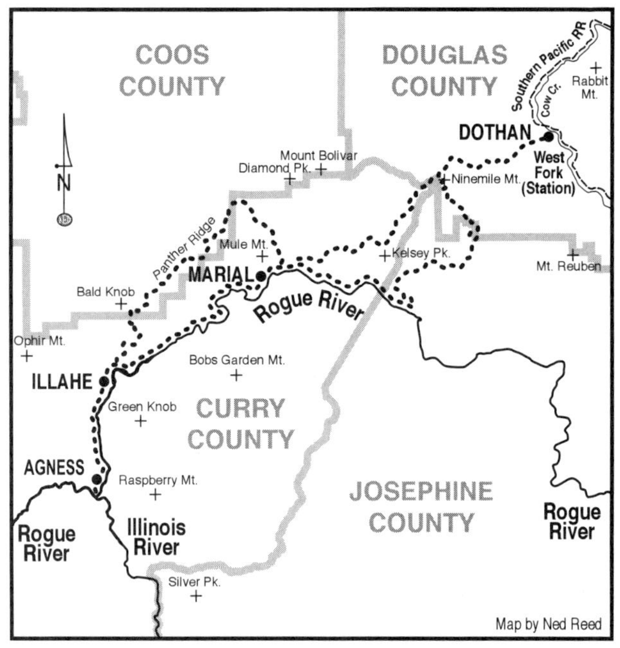

Probable routes of Hathaway Jones
Information provided by Gold Beach Ranger District, Siskiyou National Forest

Mules being loaded with mail at Marial, Oregon 1932.
Photo Courtesy Oregon Historical Society

Dedication of Patterson Memorial Bridge 1932
Photo Courtesy Curry Historical Society

Chapter 12

A PARTY FOR A BRIDGE

Patterson Memorial Bridge 1932 – the present

Jane Hansen laughed and clapped her hands in excitement. A marching band came toward her across the brand new Rogue River bridge. Hundreds of cars and a few thousand people lined the edges of the road on both ends of the bridge. Some had come from California, some from Washington, and many from other parts of Oregon. This was a big day for Gold Beach, the state of Oregon, and for California and Washington.

So much was going on, it was hard to see everything. There were boat races on the river, dancing, and games. Men gave speeches and someone cut a ribbon that stretched across the road. Jane thought that was a funny thing to do because people had been using the bridge even before it was finished, back in January.

The bridge was named for Governor Isaac Lee Patterson. He was Governor of Oregon from 1926 to 1929, and he very much wanted the bridge to be built. Patterson died before his term was over. His widow had come to the celebration.

Jane did not understand everything she heard that day, but she knew the bridge was important to people travelling along the coast. If her family wanted to drive north across the river, they had to wait for a ferry. After they drove onto the ferry, it seemed to take a long time to cross the river. With the bridge, they would be able to get across much more quickly. Her parents had said there were still four ferries on the Oregon coast, but travel was getting easier.

Jane liked being up high on the bridge. She could see such a long way up the river and out to the ocean. The bridge was beautiful to look at when a person stood on the shore at one end or the other. She counted the graceful arches that touched the water; there were seven. The date was May 28, 1932, two days before the birthday of Conde B. McCullough.

- - - - - - - - -

The Patterson Bridge over the Rogue River was a highlight in the career of designer Conde McCullough, Chief Bridge Engineer for Oregon. For the first time, he used a way of building bridges that had been used in France. The slender arches of the French design used less concrete but were very strong. The system worked very well at Gold Beach, but McCullough did not use it on any other bridges.

To build the bridge, cement and steel bars were sent by ship to Port Orford, then by truck to the river. Lumber came from local mills, mostly at Bandon. Logs for pilings came from local forests, and sand and gravel for concrete came from the river. Patterson Bridge was the largest bridge built in Oregon up to that time, and the largest on the coast highway between San Francisco and the Columbia River.

The coast highway in Oregon was begun at the north end, about the year 1914. In the early years of construction it was supposed to be a military highway to help in defense of the West Coast. It was called the "Theodore Roosevelt Military Highway." Only two miles had been paved by 1918.

In the 1920s Portlanders wanted to be able to get to the beaches and drive along the coast. In 1929 the Great Depression started and many men were out of work. Building roads and bridges made jobs. These reasons helped move the project along.

Highway crews graded and paved sections of the road, always moving southward.

They built bridges over creeks and canyons. The highway was mostly finished by 1931 when work began on the Rogue River bridge. That same year, the name was changed to Oregon Coast Highway, U. S. 101.

Four bridges were still needed and McCullough set about building them: the Umpqua River Bridge at Reedsport, Siuslaw River Bridge at Florence, Yaquina Bay Bridge at Newport, and Coos Bay Bridge. All four bridges were finished in 1936, completing the highway and ending the use of ferries. The timing was good because automobile traffic was increasing fast. The Roosevelt Ferry at Coos Bay carried 33 cars on July 4, 1922; on July 4, 1935, it carried 1,976 cars.

The bridge at Coos Bay was one of McCullough's greatest works, the longest in Oregon's highway system. At the time it was built it was the sixth longest bridge in the world. It arches high above the water so that ships can pass underneath.

In 1947 the bridge was renamed for McCullough, who had died the year before. He had spent his life studying engineering, learning from great teachers and forming his own ideas. He loved building bridges. He believed that bridges should carry traffic well and should be strong. They should not be too expensive to build, and they should be beautiful.

McCullough spent his early years in Iowa before coming to Oregon in 1916. He wanted to work where there were few roads and bridges so he could use his creative talents. He did just that. In 1980 in Oregon 3200 bridges were still in use; 900 had been built under Conde McCullough's direction.

Even sturdy concrete bridges do not last forever; on the coast there is a silent enemy—salt. In the late twentieth century highway engineers discovered that in many coastal bridges, salt had worked its way through the concrete to the reinforcing steel inside. This caused the steel to wear away, weakening the bridges and making them unsafe.

Plans were made to repair the Oregon coast bridges, using a new technology. It was too late to save the lovely Alsea Bay bridge at Waldport, and it was taken down and replaced. Several other bridges have been repaired. The McCullough Bridge is scheduled for work in 2007.

David A. Fletcher, Access Manager and Project Coordinator for the Patterson Bridge project, had the once-in-a-lifetime chance to crawl, walk, and touch every square foot of the bridge. He believes Mr. McCullough was very intelligent. Says Fletcher, "For bridge design in the 21st century we use computers to aid in the design. Back when he was designing, all the computations were done by long-hand."

"Everything was done by hand," adds Fletcher. "Logs were floated down the river for the forms and mining for the concrete rock was done in the bay. They did not have the luxury of a 9-yard concrete truck or concrete pump truck. Today we are spoiled with all our fancy equipment. They transported materials across the river with a mining cart on rails."

The Patterson Bridge project is set to be finished in 2005. The renewed bridge will be a fitting memorial for the Governor who believed it should be built and the engineer who designed it.

ENDNOTES
Chapter 12

Jane Hansen was not a real person.

The next time you are travelling on the Oregon Coast Highway, take a good look at the beautiful bridges. They blend nicely with the trees and water that make the Oregon coast such a special place. At Waldport, at the south end of the new Alsea Bay Bridge, there is an interpretive center with exhibits about the bridges and more information about Conde McCullough.

Patterson Bridge during repair work in 2004
Photo Courtesy Curry County Reporter Newspaper in Gold Beach

Chapter 13

FIRE!

Bandon Fire 1936

Tears ran down Jenny Adams' face; tears from fear and sadness and from smoke in the air. She huddled under a blanket on the sand, between her mother and father. Her dog lay nearby. Holding a wet cloth over her nose, Jenny stared across the Coquille River at the burning town of Bandon.

Brilliant orange flames lit the September night sky. The girl watched in horror as one building after another collapsed in a shower of sparks. Loud noises were all around them: the roar of the raging fire, snapping of sparks, and a boom whenever a gas tank exploded.

"Mother," she asked in panic. "Is our house gone?"

Her mother's tired voice replied, "I don't know. But it doesn't look good."

Jenny thought of her favorite things at home. She knew the most important things were here with her on the sand. Her family was safe. She snuggled closer to her mother. She put her arm around her dog, which cowered and whimpered.

The riverbank was crowded with people who had fled from the fast-moving fire. Some waited on the beach at the south jetty. Some watched in disbelief from the steamer *Alvarado* or the lighthouse tender *Rose*. Lifeboat crews from both boats ferried people to safety. The Coast Guard and the crew of the harbor tug also helped.

Volunteer firemen were working hard and the watchers could only wait until daylight. It seemed impossible to sleep, but Jenny dozed a few times. Each time she opened her eyes, she could see only fire, still burning. People were saying that a part of Bandon had burned before, in 1914. But this was no ordinary fire.

The weather had been unusually dry for weeks. In September hot, dry winds blew on the town from the east. This was not normal; people were used to cool, moist breezes blowing in from the ocean.

Some people worried about fire danger, but most went about their daily lives. In mid-September, when the temperature dropped, worry lessened. Hunters went out into the woods and logging continued.

Then, on September 26, the temperature quickly rose to 90° F. and the air became very dry, with less than 10% humidity. A fire of unknown cause started several miles east of Bandon. Fires burned in several locations and joined. Crews fought fires in several places. By late afternoon, a large fire burned close to Bandon.

People living outside of town in the path of the fires worked frantically to try to save their homes. Some families loaded cars with a few items and drove to safety. This was not easy, as fires were also burning near the towns of

Marshfield (which was called Coos Bay after 1944), Coquille, and Myrtle Point. Drivers had to pass between walls of fire in several places.

Most Bandon residents went on with their lives until later in the evening. Around 8:00 or 9:00 the word came and spread like the fire itself. At the movie theater, the picture was stopped and the fire chief spoke. He said he needed all able-bodied men to fight the fire. The chief tried to help people stay calm as they began to leave the theater. They went to their homes, gathered a few belongings, and warned their neighbors. Many men turned out to help while their families went to the beach or to the river.

Firefighters went to work with trucks and hoses. They fought hard, but they had big problems. By the time the fire reached Bandon, it was huge, hot, and hungry. Pine trees and brush burned fiercely and exploded, helping to spread the fire. Some buildings burst and started burning when no flames could be seen nearby.

The strong wind kept changing direction and there was much fuel for the fire. Some water pipes in Bandon were made of wood. So were the streets and most of the buildings. Even pumping water from the river did not help for long because the fire was too powerful. In the end, the firefighters lost the fight. The last hose burned and the truck caught fire. It was all over before dawn.

In the morning people waiting on beaches and boats looked out at a blackened emptiness where Bandon had been. Only a few charred buildings and ghostly chimneys were left standing. At least nine people had died.

Survivors had smudged faces and red eyes. Some were burned and scratched from fighting the fire or trying to escape. Families comforted each other and checked to see if anyone was missing. Help came from nearby towns: food, clothing, blankets, and first aid supplies. The Red Cross, National Guard, and other groups came to help.

Those without homes stayed away from the burned area in empty shacks or with people whose houses on the far edges of town had not burned. Some slept outdoors in fields. In a few days a new city—a city of tents—stood ready to shelter people until they could build new houses. In the days following September 26, a few more people died from effects of the fire.

Fires still burned north, south, and east of Bandon for weeks. In November, helped by rain, the fires were at last put out. No other towns in the area burned, but they narrowly escaped Bandon's fate.

Some folks moved away from Bandon, but most stayed. The town slowly began to come to life again. Houses were built and businesses started again. People went back to work and to school. Curry and Coos County residents in their seventies and eighties still tell stories about the big fire of '36.

ENDNOTES
Chapter 13

Jenny Adams was not a real person, but more than 1500 adults and children had similar experiences the awful night of September 26, 1936.

Bandon suffered a fire in 1914, when nearly three blocks of the town burned. That fire started in a restaurant, possibly in a faulty chimney, and spread to surrounding buildings.

Fire was a common problem. Native Americans told of a huge forest fire around 1850 in the Upper Coquille River area. From 1845 to 1855 there were more serious forest fires in the Coast Range than during any known period before or since. Such fires happened almost always in the late summer or early fall, after a very dry season, such as in 1936.

Port Orford was destroyed by fire in 1868, also the result of a forest fire. Marshfield had a big fire in 1922.

Early towns were built mostly of wood and early firefighting equipment was not always efficient. Some observers of the 1936 fire say it is doubtful that modern equipment could have handled it.

Bandon is now a popular stop for tourists to the Southern Oregon coast. They like to visit shops, restaurants, art galleries, candy factories, a former cheese factory, beaches, golf courses and a lighthouse.

Remains of houses the morning after fire of September 26, 1936
Photo Courtesy of the Bandon Historical Society

Tent city where people lived after their homes were burned
Photo Courtesy of the Bandon Historical Society

Chapter 14

LIFE ON THE "HOME FRONT"

World War II in Curry County 1941 - 1945

Nettie Ellis pulled back the edge of the heavy curtain at the window. She loved to see moonlight on the ocean and this was a clear night.

"Stop!" called her brother, Ted. "Don't ya know there's a war on?" We have ta keep the windows blacked out all the time so Jap planes can't see to bomb us."

Nettie sighed and let the blackout curtain fall back into place. Ted was sixteen, seven years older than Nettie, and she thought him bossy. Of course, she knew there was a "war on," but she didn't quite know what a "war" was.

It was 1942. When Japan bombed Pearl Harbor in the Hawaiian Islands in December, 1941, the United States joined a war being fought in Europe and Asia.

Germany, Italy and Japan were fighting against the Allies, which included the United States, England, France, and some other countries. Grandpa helped Nettie find all the countries on a globe. It all seemed so far away, and the Pacific Ocean was so big! Still, if the Japanese wanted to do it, they could come across all that water and attack the Oregon coast.

Nettie's family listened to the radio and read the newspaper to find out what was happening in the war. Grandpa had a world map on his bedroom wall with tiny flags on pins for Germany, Japan, and the United States. After each battle, he stuck a flag in the map for the country that won.

Ted collected pictures of war planes. The gas station gave them away; his bedroom walls were covered.

Nettie heard her parents talking about rationing. They had to have the right stamps to buy sugar, meat, and other foods. Gasoline was rationed, too, and tires and other things.

At school Nettie read about the war in *My Weekly Reader*. Sometimes she bought savings stamps. That was a way for children to help the government and have money for themselves later, when they were older. She helped with school scrap drives for tin cans or other metal. Every classroom had buckets of sand and a shovel. They were for putting out fires if the school was bombed.

Nettie felt scared when she thought about those things. It was also scary to go to the beach. Coast Guardsmen walked the beaches with big dogs in case any enemies tried to come on shore. Mostly, Nettie and her family lived their lives as best they could. They did not know when they were really in danger.

- - - - - - - - - -

Adults living at home during the war had special jobs. One job was volunteering to spend time in towers watching for airplanes and reporting anything unusual they saw. Forest rangers at fire lookouts were expected to do the extra job of spotting planes along with their regular duties. It all seemed routine until September 9, 1942.

On September 8, Japanese navy submarine I-25 was hiding under the ocean near Port Orford. Early the next morning the sub surfaced. Sailors on the deck put together a small seaplane and pilot Nobuo Fujita took off over the land. East of Brookings—between the Chetco and Winchuck Rivers—Fujita dropped fire bombs near Mt. Emily.

The plane went back to the sub, where it was taken apart and stowed; then the ship submerged.

The Japanese plan was to start a big forest fire. But lookouts at Long Ridge and Mt. Emily spotted the unusual plane and the forest was not as dry as it usually was in September, so the plan did not work. Crews were able to put out the small fires and little damage was done.

The I-25 submarine was attacked by an American plane but was not badly hurt.

The sub stayed below the surface of the ocean in the Port Orford area for some days. For at least one day, the sub lay at the bottom of the harbor. On September 29 the same small plane dropped fire bombs at Grassy Knob near Port Orford. No fires were started that time. The people of Curry County did not panic after these bombings because most people did not know they had happened. The government kept the attacks secret so that people wouldn't panic.

Before leaving the Oregon south coast, the I-25 torpedoed an American oil tanker, the Larry Doheny, near Cape Sebastian. The ship sank quickly. Forty of the forty-six men on board were quickly loaded into lifeboats. Three men died and three were listed as missing.

This time, the people of Port Orford did know about the submarine and the damage it had done. The Larry Doheny survivors were brought to the dock at Port Orford. Local people helped out with food, beds and bedding, and other things the sailors needed while they were in town.

In 1962, seventeen years after the United States won the war with Japan, the Junior Chamber of Brookings/Harbor wanted to do a project of international cooperation. Even though some local people thought it was a bad idea, the Jaycees invited Nobuo Fujita to visit Brookings and attend the Azalea Festival. The former war pilot came with his wife and son and stayed a few days. The Fujita family gave the City of Brookings their 400 year-old Samurai sword in a special ceremony. Fujita had always carried the sword on his flights. Presenting the sword to a former enemy is a pledge of peace and friendship. The sword is now displayed in the Chetco Public Library in Brookings.

ENDNOTES
Chapter 14

Nettie Ellis was not a real person. The author was a child in Washington State during World War II. People had just come out of the Great Depression and they tended to be serious much of the time during the war. Air raid drills, blackout curtains, rationing and other aspects of wartime were part of daily life.

A number of men and women from Curry County were in the armed forces during World War II. At least seventeen men were killed.

It is possible to walk to the site of the fire bombing in the forest near Mt. Emily, after driving several miles on gravel roads. A sign marks the spot.

For pictures and more information about the submarine and the bombing of Curry County, see Bert Webber's book, *Silent Siege*. Fairfield, Washington: Ye Galleon Press, 1978.

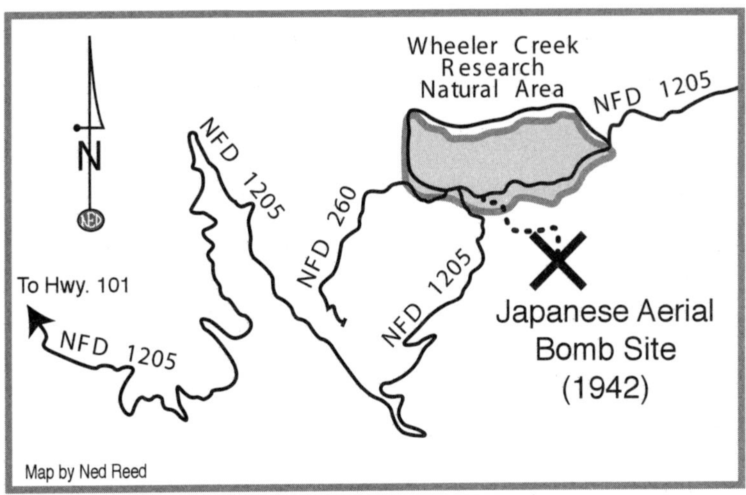

GLOSSARY

abandon – To quit or leave alone; desert.

ancestors – Relatives who lived before you, such as grandparents.

board foot – A measurement of sawn wood. One board foot is one foot (12 inches) square and one inch thick.

bog – A natural area of wet earth with decaying plants that makes a certain kind of soil.

canyon – A ditch-like formation with steep sides, usually with a river or creek at the bottom.

Chinook jargon – A made-up language used by people who have different native languages. In the Pacific Northwest, Chinook jargon was used so different Indian tribes could talk to each other and Indians and white people could talk to each other.

clipper ship – A sailing ship built for great speed.

commercial – Having to do with business; buying and selling to make money.

contract – An agreement between people A contractor agrees to do a certain job for a certain amount of money.

customs – Habits, ways of living.

dedicated – Serious about one's work or other activity.

depression – A time when many people do not have money or jobs. The United States has had several times of economic depression. The Great Depression lasted from late 1929 until about 1940.

duplex – A house divided into two living units.

erosion – Wearing away of soil by wind, water or human activity.

exposure – Being out in the cold or wet weather without protection.

freight – Goods hauled by animals, wagon, ship, train or truck.

generator – A machine that makes electricity.

humidity – The amount of moisture in the air.

industry – A kind of business.

jetty – A wall of rock and/or concrete built to protect the entrance to a harbor.

minesweeper – A warship made to clear explosive mines from the water.

natural resources – Plants and animals, the soil which makes it possible for them to live, and minerals under the ground; also, plants, animals and minerals of the streams and oceans.

ore – The basic rock that contains gold or other valuable metal.

pilings – A heavy timber driven into the earth to support a dock or bridge.

port (side of a ship) – The left side of a ship when facing ahead toward the bow.

poultry – Chickens, geese, ducks or turkeys raised on a farm.

rationing – A system for limiting scarce goods so that everyone can have some.

reef – A group of rocks in the ocean, dangerous to ships.

reservation – Land set aside by the government for a special purpose, such as a place for Native Americans to live.

riffle – An area of white water in a stream; rough for a boat but not as hard to go over as a waterfall.

sacred – Holy; respected or worshipped.

Scandinavian countries – Norway, Sweden, Denmark and Finland

schooner – A type of ship. The first were wooden sailing ships with at least two masts.

settlement – A place where people live, usually beginning with a few and growing. Some early settlements became towns or cities; some are still small villages and some disappeared. (also, the act of settling a place)

side-wheel steamer – Many steamboats in the last half of the nineteenth century had huge wooden paddles that propelled them through the water. Most had the paddle wheels at the rear of the boat, but some had wheels in the side of the boat, between bow and stern.

Siskiyou – A Native American name given to the mountainous region of southern Oregon and northern California. The name is said to mean "bob-tailed horse."

spit – A narrow point of land sticking out into a large body of water.

stranded (a ship) - Driven ashore onto the beach. A ship can strand or be stranded.

suspension bridge – A bridge supported by cables hanging from towers. The Golden Gate Bridge at San Francisco is an example of a large suspension bridge.

tall tale – A story that stretches the truth in a way that makes the story impossible to believe but humorous.

treaties – Agreements between groups of people or governments.

trinkets – Ornaments, jewelry.

turpentine – An oil made from pine trees, used as a paint thinner.

wilderness – Wild country; a desert or forest. All of what is now the United States was once wilderness.

WHAT ELSE HAPPENED? WHEN?

• **10,000 to 5,000 years ago** – Native people lived along the northwest coast of what is now the United States.

• **1848** – Oregon Territory is formed. It was a large area, including what are now Washington and Idaho, as well as Oregon. Abraham Lincoln was asked to be the first governor of the territory, but he refused. Gold is discovered at Sutter's mill in California, starting the California gold rush.

• **1851** – The first white settlement on the South Coast, at Port Orford. Gold is discovered at what is now Jacksonville, Oregon. Portland is incorporated. Rogue River Indian Wars begin and last, off and on, until 1856.

1850s – Sawmills begin on Coos Bay. Empire City and Marshfield (later Coos Bay) begin. Coal mines start operating.

1853 – Gold is discovered on black sand beaches. Coos County is formed; includes present Curry County. Washington Territory separated from Oregon Territory, with boundary at Columbia River.

1852 – Wreck of the Captain Lincoln

1854 – First sawmill in Port Orford.

1855 – Curry County is formed.

1856 – Removal of Native Americans to reservation at Siletz.

1857 – First Rogue River ferry.

1859 – Oregon becomes 33rd state in the United States.

• **1860** – Abraham Lincoln elected President of the United States.

1861 – 1865 – U. S. Civil War

1863 – Ellensburg (later Gold Beach) is formed. The town is named for Captain Tichenor's daughter.

1864 – First salmon cannery in U. S.

1866 – First lighthouse built at Cape Arago

1868 – A large forest fire destroys Port Orford.

1869 – Transcontinental railroad finished.

• **1870** – Cape Blanco Lighthouse built

1871 – United States Life-Saving Service started on the East Coast

1876 – Alexander Graham Bell invents the telephone. First Oregon capitol burns.

1877 – R. D. Hume opens a salmon cannery on the Rogue River.

1878 – First Coos Bay Life-Saving Station

• **1880** – Thomas Edison introduces the electric light. (A. W. Swan, by himself, also perfects an electric light.) Electricity does not come to the South Coast until the next century.

1881 – Blasting begins at Tupper Rock.

1883 – Transcontinental railroad reaches Portland.

1885 – First cranberries are planted on the South Coast.

1888 – The Eastman Kokak camera is introduced.

1889 – *Alaskan* shipwreck

• **1890** – The town of Ellensburg is renamed Gold Beach.

1892 – The United States Life-Saving Service builds a station at the mouth of the Coquille River (Bandon).

1893 – first Henry Ford automobile built

1895 – Mail boat service is started on the Rogue River.

1895 – Guglielmo Marconi invents the telegraph.

1898 – Hathaway Jones starts his own mail route in the Rogue River canyon. The 1800s were called "the century of steam;" the 1900's would be called "the century of electricity."

• **1903** – Wilbur and Orville Wright make the first successful airplane flight. First coast-to-coast crossing of the American continent by car, in 65 days

1904 – American work on the Panama Canal begins.

1906 – San Fancisco earthquake

1907 – Boy Scouts founded

1909 – second Cape Arago lighthouse built

• **1910** – *Czarina* shipwreck

1914 – Panama Canal finished and opened to ship traffic (Ships no longer had to sail "around the Horn" to get from Asia and the U.S. West Coast to the East Coast or to Europe.)

1914 – World War I begins.

1917 – United States enters war.

1918 – World War I ends.

• **1920's** – Coast highway built (now U.S. 101)

1926 -- 16mm movie film introduced

1927 – Charles Lindbergh's flight across the Atlantic Ocean

1928 – First television broadcasts; color movie film and color television in use

1929 – Beginning of the Great Depression

• **1932** – Patterson Bridge finished over Rogue River at Gold Beach

1934 – Third Cape Arago lighthouse

1935 – Oregon capitol burns.

1936 – Bandon burns.

1937 – Golden Gate Bridge opens.

1938 – Ballpoint pen invented in Hungary.

1939 – World War II begins in Europe.

• **1940** – Helicopters introduced

1941 – U.S. enters war

1942 – Curry County is bombed.

1942 – First computer in the U.S. , First U.S. jet plane

1944 –Town of Marshfield renamed Coos Bay

1945 – World War II ends

BIBLIOGRAPHY

Suggestions to teachers and others for further reading

This is a partial list of the books the author read or consulted in writing this book. Some might be out of print. Some might be found only in museums or libraries. Books marked with * might be of special interest to children. A complete bibliography is available from the author by request.

Atwood, Kay. *Illahe* (The Story of Settlement in the Rogue River Canyon). Medford, Oregon: Gandee Printing Center, 1978 (A newer edition is available.)

*Bandon Centennial Book Commission, 1989. *Bandon Then and Now.*

*Beckham, Curt. *The Night Bandon Burned.* Myrtle Point, Oregon (no date)

Beckham, Dow. *Bandon By-the-Sea.* Coos Bay, Oregon: Arago Books, 1997

___________ . *Stars in the Dark*: Coal Mines of Southwestern Oregon. Coos Bay, Oregon: Arago Books, 1995

*Beckham, Stephen Dow. Editor, *Tall Tales from the Rogue River* (*The Yarns of Hathaway Jones*). Bloomington, Indiana: Indiana University Press, 1974 Reprinted Oregon State University Press, Corvallis, 1990 (Note: Stephen Beckham has written and/or contributed to many excellent books of history of this region.)

*Clark, Ella E. *Indian Legends of the Pacific Northwest.* Berkeley, California: University of California Press, 1953

Coquille Indian Tribe. *Changing Landscapes* Proceedings of the 5th and 6th annual Coquille Cultural Preservation Conferences. North Bend, Oregon, 2002

DeLony, Eric. *Landmark American Bridges.* in association with American Society of Civil Engineers. Boston: Little, Brown & Co. Bullfinch Press 1993

Dodds, Gordon B. *The Salmon King of Oregon.* Chapel Hill, North Carolina: Univ. of No. Carolina Press, 1959

Dodge, Orville. *Pioneer History of Coos and Curry Counties.* Coos-Curry Pioneer and Historical Association 1969 (2nd Ed.)

Douthit, Nathan. *The Coos Bay Region 1880-1944* (Life on a Coastal Frontier). Coos Bay, Oregon: River West Books, 1981

___________ . *A Guide to Oregon's South Coast History.* Corvallis, Oregon: Oregon State University Press, 1999

Eck, Paul, *The American Cranberry.* New Brunswick, New Jersey: Rutgers University Press, 1990

Gaston, Joseph. *A Centennial History of Oregon* 1811 – 1912. Vol. IV. Chicago: S. J. Clarke Publishing Co., 1912

Gibbs, Jim. *Disaster Log of Ships*. New York: Bonanza Books, Superior Publishing Co., 1971

*Gintzler, A. S. *Rough and Ready Loggers*. Santa Fe, New Mexico: John Muir Publications, 1994

Hadlow, Robert. *Elegant Arches, Soaring Spans. C. B. McCullough Oregon's Master Bridge Builder.* Corvallis, Oregon: Oregon State University Press, 2001

Hall, Roberta. *People of the Coquille Estuary*. Corvallis, Oregon: Words & Pictures Unlimited, 1995

*Jaspersohn, William. *Cranberries*. Boston: Houghton Mifflin Co., 1991

*LeScal, Yves. *The Great Days of the Cape Horners*.Translated by L. Ortzen London: Souvenir Press, 1964 American Edition New American Library 1967

Marshall, Don. *Oregon Shipwrecks*. Portland, Oregon: Binford & Mort, 1984

McArthur, Lewis A. *Oregon Geographic Names*. Portland, Oregon: Oregon Historical Society Press, 1992

Meier, Gary and Gloria. *Whitewater Mailmen* (The Story of the Rogue River Mail Boats). Bend, Oregon: Maverick Publications, 1995

*Nelson, Sharlene and Ted. *Oregon Lighthouses*. Seattle, Washington: Umbrella Books, Epicenter Press, 1994

*O'Donnell, Terence. *That Balance So Rare* (The Story of Oregon). Portland, Oregon: Oregon Historical Society Press, 1988

Oregon Historical Society and Oregon Department of Transportation. *Historic Highway Bridges of Oregon*. 1985

Oregon State University, *Trees to Know in Oregon*. 1950

Osborne, Ernest L. *Wooden Ships and Master Craftsmen*. Bandon, Oregon: Bandon Historical Society, 1978

*_______________ and Victor West. *Men of Action* (A History of the U. S. Life-Saving Service on the Pacific Coast). Bandon, Oregon: Bandon Hist. Soc. Press, 1981

Pacific Coast Cranberry Research Foundation. *Pacific Coast Cranberries*. Long Beach, Washington 1997

Peterson, Emil, and Alfred Powers. *A Century of Coos and Curry*. Coquille, Oregon: Coos-Curry Pioneer & Historical Society, 1952

Quick, John. *Fool's Hill* (A Kid's Life in an Oregon Coastal Town). Corvallis, Oregon: Oregon State University Press, 1995

Reichenbach, Ethel Kranick. *The Life of a Cranberry Grower*. New York: Vantage Press, 1981

Robbins, William G. *Hard Times in Paradise*. Seattle, Washington: University of Washington Press, 1988

Schroeder, Walt. *Curry County Agriculture: The People and the Land*. Kearney, Nebraska: Morris Publishing, 1998

___________ . *They Found Gold on the Beach* (A History of Central Curry County). Kearney, Nebraska: Morris Publishing, 1999

Smith, Dwight A., James B. Norman, and Pieter T. Dykman. *Historic Highway Bridges of Oregon*. Portland, Oregon: Oregon Historical Society Press, 1989

*Stevens, Sydney. *C is for Cranberries*. Oysterville, Washington 1998

Stone, Boyd. *Living in the Past Lane*. Coquille, Oregon: Coquille Valley Sentinel, 1993

_________. *The Way it Really Was in Coos and Curry Counties*. Coquille, Oregon: Coquille Valley Sentinel, 1993

_________. *You are the Star*s (History of the Coquille River Area). Myrtle Point, Oregon: Myrtle Point Printing, 1995

Webber, Bert. *The Hero of Battle Rock*. Fairfield, Washington: Ye Galleon Press, 1978

___________. *Silent Siege*, Fairfield, Washington: Ye Galleon Press, 1984

Wells, R. E. and Victor C. West. *A Guide to Shipwreck Sites Along the Oregon Coast*. North Bend, Oregon 1984

Youst, Lionel. *She's Tricky Like Coyote*. Norman, Oklahoma: University of Oklahoma Press, 2002

___________, and William R. Seaburg. *Coquelle Thompson, Athabascan Witness*. Norman, Oklahoma: Univ. of Oklahoma Press, 2002

OTHER SOURCES

Pamphlets, Brochures

The Legend of Face Rock. Kronenberg, Ottile Parker. Bandon Historical Society Press, Bandon, Oregon 1997

Fire! Bandon Historical Society Press (no author or date credited)

2 brochures from The Confederated Tribes of Siletz Indians Siletz, Oregon

1 brochure from the Coquille Indian Tribe, Coos Bay, Oregon

Brochure and photos from Collier State Park and Logging Museum near Chiloquin, Oregon

Brochures from Historic Alsea Bay Bridge Interpretive Center

1 sheet of historical information from Coast Guard Station Coos Bay

Material from Oregon Parks and Recreation Department about Cape Blanco Lighthouse

July 1996 newsletter of Point Orford Heritage Society, Port Orford
October 2000 Newsletter of POHS
March 2003 Newsletter of POHS
February 2004 Newsletter of POHS

Magazine Articles

In *Oregon Coast Magazine* September/October 1991 issue:
Fleagle, Judy, and other authors "Coast Fires of 1936"
Price, Juanita, "Cranberry Festival"
__________ November/December 1991:
Marshall, Don, "The Deadly Beauty of the Sea"

Newspaper Articles

• *Portland Oregonian* June 21, July 5, 12, August 16, 1851 (regarding the ship, *Sea Gull*, and the Battle Rock incidents of Chapter 2.)
• *Oregon Statesman* June 25, 1851, also Battle Rock incidents July 4, 1851
• *Coos Bay Times* September 27, 1936 (extra edition) regarding Bandon fire
• *Coos Bay World* October 31, 1997 regarding 1700 tsunami (George Tibbits, writer)
• *Bandon Western World* October 1, 1936 regarding fire
• *Curry County Reporter*, fall 1993, article about Robert Kentta of Confederated Tribes of Siletz Indians, quoting oral history of natives. Reported by Marge Barrett
• *Port Orford News*, June 24, 1998, article by John Quick

• Obituary of James Hughes, fall 1929. Hughes House file at Port Orford Public library. Newspaper not identified.

Interviews

Telephone interview with stepgranddaughters of Hathaway Jones, Laverna Rowland and Lajuana Jarrell. October 2002

Telephone interview with Ester Conley, forest fire lookout in 1942 March 2005

Telephone interview with Martin Callery, Manager of Port of Coos Bay February 2002

Email exchange with David Fletcher of Oregon Department of Transportation April – May 2005

Museums

Bandon Historical Society, Bandon, Oregon
Coos County Historical & Maritime Museum, North Bend, Oregon
Coos County Logging Museum, Myrtle Point
Curry Historical Society, Gold Beach
Port Orford Lifeboat Station Museum, Port Orford, Oregon

Internet

Material from Port of Coos Bay

Reference to sailing ship, *Western Shore*, (from page 20, *Marine History of the Northwest*, Tacoma, Washington Public Library)

Other

Center for Population Research, Portland
Curry County marriage records
Port Orford Public Library
United States Forest Service, Siskiyou National Forest, Gold Beach Ranger District
World Book Encyclopedia,Vol. 14 page 848, article on Oregon Chicago 2001
_______________Vol. 17
1996 Map by Ned Reed showing areas of fires in 1936

In addition to the maps in this book, other maps could be helpful to anyone wanting to locate places where the stories take place:

Map of Coos County
Map of Curry County
Official state highway map of Oregon (Oregon Dept. of Transportation)
Map of Siskiyou National Forest

MAIL ORDER INFORMATION

Copies of this book may be ordered by sending a check or money order to:

Shirley Nelson
P. O. Box 1471
Port Orford, Oregon 97465

Fill out and clip the coupon below or photocopy this page and send with payment.

Please send me ______ copies of
What Happened Here? at \$14.75
per copy. This includes \$12.95
plus \$1.80 for shipping and handling.

Name ________________________________

Address ______________________________

City _________________________________

State _______________________ Zip _______